# End of the Empire

*How to protect yourself during The Collapse*

by

Michael K. Burns

I0486497

# Table of Contents

———

# About The Author

===

MIKE BURNS HAS AN MSEE, control systems from OSU and has worked for 35 years in the defense industry primarily doing missile guidance. Always a student of history, Mike uses his free time in retirement to turn his attention toward the decline of the US. He spends his days living a modest and minimalist lifestyle in Texas with his son, father, and cat Peanut, or in Los Angeles visiting his two daughters and various friends. When not in the US, he travels around the world immersing himself in foreign cultures. Mike draws inspiration from many authors including Robert Greene, Ayn Rand, Michael Lewis and Robert Wringer.

# Introduction

———

EMPIRES COME AND GO. We are just specs of dust in an unimaginably vast and unimaginably old universe. People are short-lived and few of us read history, so our sense of permanence leads us to believe that things will always continue as they have for the past 20-30 years. Most stars burn out in a few billion years, though some very small ones are theorized to last up to a trillion years. These earthly empires are both tiny and brief and they follow a more or less predictable arc of rising, plateauing and eventually declining.

This book is about the decline of the United States, how it's already happening, what is likely to happen next, the causes of The Collapse (as history books will refer to it in 50 years) and what to do in order to mitigate the impact to yourself and your family. Here's only a partial list of some past empires that most people expected would never end:

Achaemenid (Persian): 500 BC - 330 BC, high point 500 BC

Greek (Macedon): 808 BC-168 BC, high point 323 BC

Roman: 509 BC – 456 AD; high point 180 AD

Spanish: 1492 – 1898, high point 1580

Dutch: 1590 – 1710, high point 1688

British: 1700 - 1956, high point 1914

When we read history we find that most of these empires were, at their peak, the undisputed leaders of the world. And each exhibited approximately the same sort of behaviors, and same multi-faceted decline, as we are now witnessing in the United States. The dates above

3

are all approximate and the empires suffered declines long before the listed end dates.

For example, the Spanish empire lost many of their new-world colonies in the early 1800's, but I have chosen 1898 as their definitive end date because in that year the US would crush them in the Spanish-American war, taking the Philippines and Cuba. Similarly, the British empire was in decline even before WWII, but I've chosen 1956 as the demise based on their humiliating loss in the Suez Crisis, which followed the loss of the crown jewel of the empire, India, in 1948. One conclusion we can draw from looking at many past empires is that being dominant today does not guarantee being dominant forever.

I expect that entrenched politicians and their billionaire-controlled media pundits will almost universally try to discredit me because this book lays most of the blame at the feet of cynical politicians. Any person or group who speaks against the established power structure is quickly discredited by the media machine. No trial or even facts are necessary. I'll be called racist, reactionary, liberal, unpatriotic or a Russian mole; whatever words can be used to try to keep people away from my ideas. Oscar Wilde put it well when he said *"If you cannot prove a man wrong, don't panic. You can always call him names."*

But there's truly a lot of pain in middle-America that's being masked by the many gamed statistics (unemployment, underemployment, consumer price index, and non-existent wage growth) put out by the US government. The bogus statistics have been published by the US Government (e.g. BLS.gov) under both Democrat and Republican presidents, so there's plenty of blame to go around.

The pain is occasionally manifested in unexpected ways such as Donald Trump's shocking underdog win in the 2016 US presidential election. You might recall that on the eve of the election, every major poll and every major news organization were predicting that Hillary Clinton would have an easy and sweeping victory, with probability around 90%. It's natural that the news media would predict Hillary winning since it's well-known that people like to feel like they're going along with the crowd. It's a strong incentive to vote for Hillary if the news media tells you that the vast majority of other people are voting for her too. It's like an undercover kind of free advertising by CNN, MSNBC and NPR for their preferred candidate.

In the 2020 election, we'll again witness the news media predicting Trump's loss, and for the same reasons. But if you're reading this book, maybe you can look beyond the propaganda in the so-called "mainstream media". Read onward, look up the statistics yourself, then make up your own mind. As David Bowie put it: *"Tomorrow belongs to those who can hear it coming"* [69].

# Chapter 1

# It Can't Happen Here (Spoiler: It already is)

=====

A LOT OF PEOPLE ON the right and on the left don't want to hear the truth and will fight hard to ignore it. People will tune into radio, TV and internet based stories to confirm their present beliefs, rather than seeking to be informed. Most people want a comfortable existence without having to stress out or put too much thought into things. To paraphrase Nietzsche: *"If you want to know what the average person will do in any given situation, just find the choice that requires the least amount of thought."*[1]

But if we are on the precipice of a sickening decline, then that would be scary to most people and would require a lot of thought to try to mitigate the damage. It would be easier to be like Straker in the movie *The Matrix*, ignoring all of that unpleasant reality and escaping to the happy place of hedonism and lies.

Coming to grips with the end of an empire and the big changes in your own lifestyle is certainly hard. It's much like accepting the death of someone close to you, maybe your parent or child. At first, most people will deny it. "No, this isn't happening. Everything will be fine." And there will be plenty of cheerleader politicians who say that everything is fine, that people are being too negative in pointing out the decline, and even that it's unpatriotic to speak against the US.

In this chapter we're going to look at some statistics that show how the US is not merely stagnating, but moving backwards in many key areas. Yes, we were number one in almost every area just a decade or two ago, but now we're going downhill. We'll also examine how important statistics coming out of the government are gamed to make things look better and rob us of the ability to get an impartial comparison to past years.

It came as a shock to most Americans in 2014 to learn that life expectancy actually declined that year [2]. Politicians and news media quickly labeled it a quirk or said that it was just statistical noise. Recall that this was during the first term of President Obama, and we were told that everything was now wonderful and that the country had "hope", that things were progressing like never before. But then it happened again in 2016, and shocked people when it happened a third time in 2017. These declines were relatively small but they were still a reversal of the trend of ever-increasing life expectancies in the US.

How could this possibly happen, and under the watch of the Nobel Prize winning Godly Man no less? In nearly every other industrial and technologically advanced country, life expectancies had been rising, modestly but steadily, for generations. Only during such extreme events as wartime, revolution, and genocide did any other countries see their life expectancies decline.

One of the very few examples of falling life expectancies from recent history is from the USSR in the early 1990's [32]. Their life expectancy fell from over 69 years to around 64. Here's a bit of the history: President Reagan had engaged the USSR in a defense race which the USSR just couldn't afford. The Russian economy was already creaking under the Stalinesque inefficiency of their heavy-handed central planning, and they had no hope to try to keep up with the US "Star Wars" buildup.

But their masters in the Kremlin tried to somewhat keep pace with the Americans, and so the Russian economy collapsed and their various Eastern European satellite states like East Germany, Poland and

Ukraine all broke away and formed their own governments (and embarrassingly, close defense ties to the US).

Life in Russia was miserable and many people turned to the national beverage: vodka. Some die-hard communist apologists even blamed their collapse on alcoholism. In reality the alcoholism was merely a symptom. Most people were feeling defeated and hopeless because they were impoverished and not free to even try to make things better.

Some people in the US blamed the "opioid epidemic" on the increased deaths from 2015-2017. Some went so far as to accuse China of chemical warfare by sending tons of the highly addictive and deadly narcotic Fentanyl to the US. But just like blaming vodka for Russia's collapse, it was merely a symptom of the peoples' misery, and not the cause.

People have had access to all manner of different drugs for many decades before Fentanyl. In the early 1900's people could buy pure heroin at the drug store without a prescription. We had the crack epidemic and the meth epidemic. Every few years the War on Drugs was re-branded with a new demon, but it didn't really change.

What did change was that the US economy was slowly sinking and bringing despair to more millions of people, though these people were carefully hidden from the evening news on CNN. Instead, we were told repeatedly how inflation was incredibly low, even though the prices of food, housing, medical care and education were all increasing much faster than the quoted Consumer Price Index.

One indication of why the misery in the US has steadily increased is that the standard of living has gone down. Many other countries have pulled ahead of the US during the Bush-Obama years [3]. In 1980 the US ranked as the first country in the world, but by 2020 the US had the 12th highest standard of living, and going lower with each passing year. Before this decline, the US had the undisputed highest standard of living in the world, but we've been moving backwards.

Even though computerization is making workers become much more productive, we're actually seeing our standard of living decline due to reduced wages and increased prices. All of the increases from improved productivity have gone to the top 0.1%. When we look at real wages, adjusted for the actual inflation rate [4a] we can see in Figure 1 how wages actually fell when we account for inflation being higher than the official numbers put out by the US government.

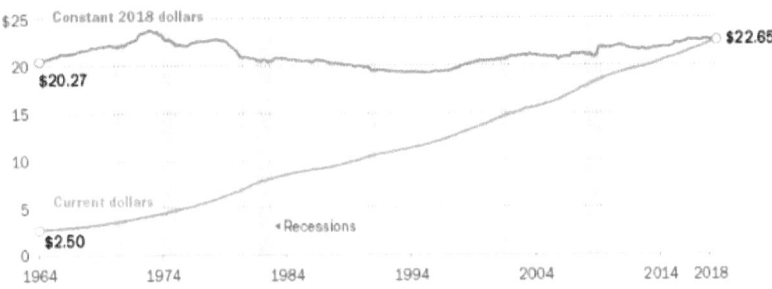

**Americans' paychecks are bigger than 40 years ago, but their purchasing power has hardly budged**

*Average hourly wages in the U.S., seasonally adjusted*

Note: Data for wages of production and non-supervisory employees on private non-farm payrolls. "Constant 2018 dollars" describes wages adjusted for inflation. "Current dollars" describes wages reported in the value of the currency when received. "Purchasing power" refers to the amount of goods or services that can be bought per unit of currency.
Source: U.S. Bureau of Labor Statistics.

**PEW RESEARCH CENTER**

Figure 1: Real wages after adjusting for inflation, from the Pew Research Center

Note that the real wages, adjusted for inflation (green line at the top) are based on the government's own estimate of inflation. More on how that's gamed later, but if we use more realistic inflation data such as in figure 2 below, then the real wages have actually fallen from 1978.

During the Clinton years, there was tremendous pressure to show that things were getting better, and so to answer this call the Federal Reserve slavishly adjusted how they calculated the Consumer Price Index. For example, as people grow poorer, they substitute hamburger for steak. Hamburger is cheaper, and so the official numbers compare the present price of hamburger to the previous price of steak, magically showing a decrease in price for that segment, which canceled out increases in other segments. But this approach is a lie meant to hide the true inflation rate.

The organization Shadowstats has been calculating inflation [6] by using the previous (and fairer) method. Figure 2 shows the true inflation rate [4b] over the years, comparing it to the official measure put out by the US government. During the years 1980 to 2020, the median price of housing went up from 55k to 223k, or by 480% [4c] and food costs exceeded the CPI as well. Note that housing and food are typically the two largest parts of a family's budget, and these costs rose much faster than wages.

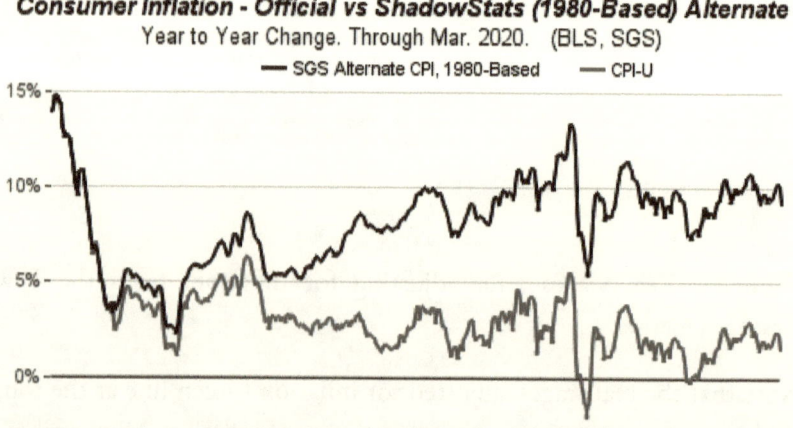

**Consumer Inflation - Official vs ShadowStats (1980-Based) Alternate**
Year to Year Change. Through Mar. 2020.   (BLS, SGS)
— SGS Alternate CPI, 1980-Based      — CPI-U

Published: Apr. 10, 2020                                    ShadowStats.com

Figure 2: Inflation rate (CPI) as computed by Shadowstats.com

———

ANOTHER WAY THE GOVERNMENT misleads us into believing that things are rosier than they are is by gaming the unemployment statistics and systematically under-counting how many people are actually unemployed. The official US government unemployment statistics [5] are shown in figure 3. The widely-reported unemployment rate has fallen steadily for 10 years, so everything is wonderful right?

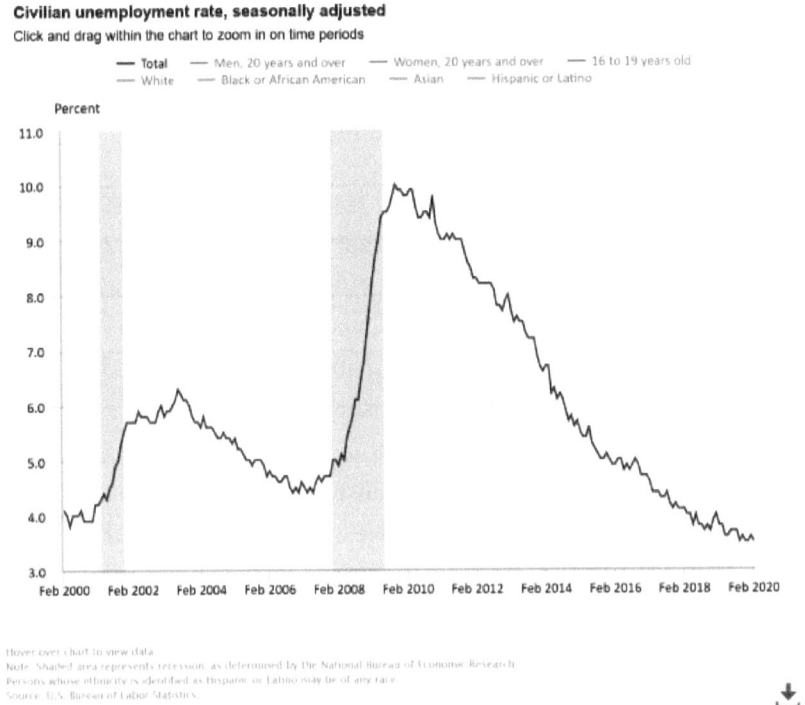

Figure 3: US Unemployment Rate Over Time, from BLS.gov.

But then from the same US government website, we also have the labor participation rate, as shown in figure 4.

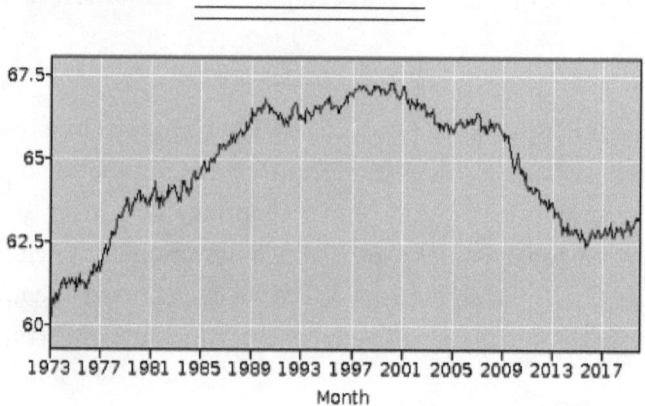

FIGURE 4: US LABOR Participation Rate, from BLS.gov.

The Labor Participation Rate (LPR) is the percent of all working age people who actually have a job. It's now (2020) close to the lowest that it's been since the 1970's. The only reason that it was this low in the 1970's is that there were still many traditional families where one person (usually the man) worked and one person stayed at home. Since then, we've become so impoverished that now it takes two people working to have the same standard of living as could be obtained with one earner in the 1970's. Why? Because housing, medicine, food and education have all increased in price much faster than the official Consumer Price Index.

The mainstream news usually doesn't discuss the Labor Participation Rate because it's embarrassing, even though the official Bureau of Labor Statistics (BLS.gov) publishes it alongside the unemployment numbers each month. The reason it's ignored is that it tends to make people ask uncomfortable questions and draw conclusions that our masters in DC would like to avoid.

On the few occasions when CNBC or CNN will talk about the Labor Participation Rate, they'll be quick to interview some self-proclaimed "expert". This is usually an academic from an Ivy League school, to make it palatable to the masses. For example, they'll usually say *"The low LPR is merely because so many old people are retiring now and living such long, happy and prosperous lives."* This argument isn't hard to refute.

Earlier we noted that the life expectancy had stagnated and even dropped for several years. And the zero interest rate policy (ZIRP) of the Fed has meant that old people's investments pay close to nothing now. The result of this is that people are working longer and longer now than they ever have before. The retirement age has been creeping upward for several years (despite the same or lower life expectancies) [42].

Between 2002 and 2020, the average retirement age of Americans has increased from 59 to 65 years. This isn't because we're living 7 years longer or because we're so much wealthier. People are working longer because they're poorer and lack the money to retire as early as they did 20 years ago.

State unemployment officials are under a lot of pressure to make the unemployment rates lower and lower. There are multiple reasons for this. Politicians in power don't want to see headlines such as "Unemployment Rate under Governor Jones has increased from 5% to 6%". Also, the fewer people who are on unemployment means that the state government has to pay out less money. So, the unemployment officials try to keep people off the unemployment rolls and kick off the ones who do manage to jump through all of the many hoops and pass all of the official tests.

Businesses have a big incentive not to officially "lay off" workers. It's better to fire workers for an official cause because then the person can't claim unemployment. If someone is laid off and files for unemployment benefits, then that business is penalized with higher unemployment taxes. A friend of mine has a daughter who worked in a popular chain restaurant as a bartender. She always got favorable reviews and made decent tips from her satisfied customers. Everyone was happy: management, customers and the waitress herself enjoyed the benefit of her hard work. But the bar was sold and a new manager came in. This new manager had lots of his own people whom he wanted to bring along to work in the restaurant, so he fired all of the old people.

Of course, he had to fabricate a reason why all of the old waitstaff were doing poorly. He reported that all of people had been performing poorly and were insubordinate. The unemployment officials dutifully noted the poor performance, sided with the business, and denied unemployment claims to all of those people who were thrown out of work. The business was happy because it didn't have to pay the higher unemployment tax rate. The government officials were happy because they kept the unemployment rate low and didn't have to pay out benefits.

The evening news people gushed that the unemployment was the best that it had been in decades. Everyone was happy. Well, almost everyone was happy, except for those "deadbeats" who had lost their jobs, but of course the evening news ignored those lost souls. It would be a downer to talk about them, so they were officially non-existent.

Related to the problem of unemployment is that a lot of young people are going to college and then are unable to get any job with their degree. Part of the problem is just the weak state of the economy in general. And part of the problem lays with school guidance counselors who tell kids "Don't worry about the money. Just do what you love and the money will come to you." But there are some people who just love to smoke weed and lay on the couch watching cartoons all day. Money is not likely to ever come to these people.

Those with degrees in art history, gender studies, philosophy and sociology also find that almost no one wants to pay them money to spout gender nonsense or philosophize. It's true that a few of these people will go on to get a PhD and they can get desirable jobs teaching in colleges, but most people with a bachelor's degree in those subjects will not get a PhD. More likely, they'll be unemployed for a long time and live in their parents' basement. After a certain amount of time doing that, they'll eventually get a job as a waiter or bartender (serving many of their friends who studied medicine, engineering, programming or business).

But many of these young people are very unhappy about their lives and about being lied to by guidance counselors so they end up hating "the system". These people are then easily recruited by groups like ANTIFA or socialists who tell them that their problem is a "failure of capitalism". This contributes to the demographic shift that's pushing the country to be very left wing and destructive of the economy. It's a bit ironic that leftists have told the kids to follow the path of "doing what you love" and yet rather than be angry at the leftists they're angry at those who work and make this country wealthier.

It would be better if school guidance counselors would give kids honest advice about what sorts of jobs their skills would be valuable for, and then show them the average salaries of those jobs after 5 or 10 years. Then young people would be able to make an informed decision about the trade-off: money or a fun job. Maybe you'd like to do gender studies, but find that it pays nothing, so you go on and get a degree in English and teach high school. This gives enough money to be able to have a decent life, an apartment, a car and a few luxuries. Ignoring the trade-off doesn't make it go away. It just means that you probably get the worst trade-off and a miserable life.

Another huge problem that we have is the national debt and how much it costs to just pay the interest. Figure 5 below shows how the debt has grown in recent years.

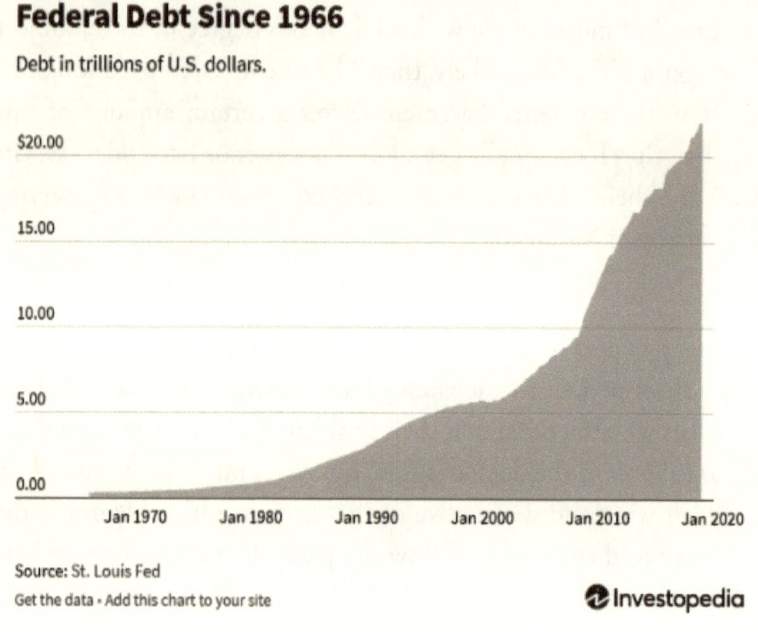

**Federal Debt Since 1966**

Debt in trillions of U.S. dollars.

Source: St. Louis Fed

Get the data · Add this chart to your site                    **Investopedia**

Figure 5: US National Debt, from Investopedia

During the administration of George W. Bush, the debt approximately doubled from $4 trillion to $8 trillion [4e] (about 9% per year). During the Obama administration, it more than doubled from $8 trillion to $20 trillion (about 12% per year). So far, after the first 4 years of the Trump administration, it was increased from $20 trillion up to $23.5 trillion, an increase of less than 20% (or 4.5% per year) as of the time I'm writing (March, 2020).

If these rates continue, the debt under Trump will have increased by a factor of about 1.5, which is better than the 2 under Bush and 2.5 under Obama, but it's still unworkable. Even though the increases under

Trump are a smaller percentage than Bush or Obama, the debt is still growing much faster than the economy. This means that the debt is growing at a rate that is faster than the ability of the government to pay it.

When Bush took over in 2000, the national debt was about 60% of the GDP. When he left office and Obama took over in 2008, the debt was about 80% of GDP. By the time Obama left office, the debt/GDP ratio was about 100%. This all means that the debt is growing much faster than our economy, so the government tax revenue will have a harder and harder time covering the interest. Currently, the debt is about 107% of the GDP.

If you followed the Greek debt crisis from about 2010-present, you'll recall that Greece's problems started when their debt was about 110% of GDP, so we're close to that now and may have already exceeded it by the time you read this. The US has advantages that Greece didn't have, so we can probably go on for longer before our crisis point hits, but that doesn't mean we can delay the day of reckoning forever.

One advantage that we have is that the US dollar is the world's reserve currency, meaning that banks all over the world hold US dollars (as well as gold and, increasingly, Euros) as a form of collateral. Also, the US dollar is used to facilitate trade between countries. Oil is priced in dollars, so even if China wants to buy from Kuwait, they use the dollar as the intermediate currency of exchange. Many powerful and wealthy people and governments have strong vested interests to hope that the US doesn't become insolvent. But amicable hopes can only carry us so far when it comes to handling this debt.

Even now, banks and governments are starting to switch to carrying more Euros and gold and less dollars. China and Russia have been in talks that are aimed at getting away from having oil priced in dollars.

Important leaders around the world can see that the US is in danger, and are therefore making contingency plans for when the US crashes.

When talking about the debt to GDP ratio being at 107% and increasing for the US, many people like to bring up the example of Japan who has a miserable debt of about 250% of GDP. The implication is that we can go a long time, maybe 30 years, before it becomes a problem. However, Japan is very different from the US. And even though Japan has thus far been able to service their debt, the rest of their economy has suffered horrendously for having run up such a debt. They have had very low growth because the government soaks up a huge amount of investment that could be used to build factories and other productive assets.

It's become very difficult for Japanese to get decently paying jobs and it's quite common there for young people to continue to live with their parents well into their 30's and beyond because they can't afford to ever buy their own house or condo. Young couples can't afford to start a family and so Japan's birth rate is far below what's needed to keep their population stable. As their population declines, then their GDP will decline too, giving progressively worse debt/GDP in coming years.

You might remember when Japan in the 1970's was the envy of all their neighbors. They had bounced back from WWII (due to having a market economy forced on them by General MacArthur) and were selling vast numbers of high quality and low priced cars to the US. Even by the early 1990's they were still doing well and the US was imitating Japan's Total quality Management and Just in Time systems. But they have fallen a long way due to the ruinous effects of Keynesian economics and trying to print money as a way of stimulating their economy. Imitating Japan will surely crush our economy as well.

Also, Japan sells their debt almost entirely to their own people. The Japanese are very homogeneous and patriotic, so they're willing to take

0% interest on the debt as way to be patriotic. But the US sells most of their debt to foreign countries (primarily China and Japan). These foreign countries are looking for stability and a reasonable rate of return, and are not driven by patriotism to help us. We can't count on them buying our debt when the debt to GDP reaches high levels and it becomes risky to hold US bonds for fear of inflation or even cancellation of the US national debt. Therefore I believe that the US will have their breaking point much sooner than Japan has, i.e. at a lower debt/GDP ratio, probably around 2025 when the debt/GDP reaches about 130% and people lose faith in the ability of the US to pay.

But you might be saying "What about Trump? He's reforming the economy, cutting taxes and will make things better." While it's true that Trump is doing the right things such as cutting taxes on the middle-class and corporations, creating jobs and reducing over-regulation, it just isn't enough. He inherited an unworkable system with built-in increases in spending. Maybe the GDP will increase by an extra 1% or 2% per year, from 2% GDP growth to 4%, if things are really great. But the national debt is increasing roughly 10% per year. There is no way for the GDP to catch up with the debt, and therefore the debt to GDP will continue to get worse at increasing rates.

It's as though we're in a bus driving down the highway at 75mph. We find ourselves headed directly toward a sheer cliff only 20 feet away. It doesn't matter if we hit the brakes or swerve. It's too late for that. We're still going over the edge. Even though Trump is doing the right things, it simply delays the inevitable. This gives you a bit more time to prepare, but not much.

Another worrisome trend, showing the overall decline of the US, is how our press freedoms and freedom of speech is getting worse. In fact, the US only ranks at 45 [7] in press freedom worldwide in 2019. This is down from 20$^{th}$ place in 2010. There are various reasons for this decline. Courts have sided with police to force reporters to give out the names of whistle-blowers. We've seen the prosecution of Julian Assange of WikiLeaks and Edward Snowden specifically because they revealed corruption of the US government and the Democratic Party.

We have various hate-speech laws making it increasingly difficult to talk openly about Islamic terrorist attacks such as the attack on the French magazine *Charlie Hebdo* in 2015. Politicians, including Al Gore, have suggested having laws against so-called "climate-change deniers". Donald Trump and Nancy Pelosi have both suggested various punishments for "fake news" (usually defined as any news that differs from what they consider to be true).

Then there are the many unofficial punishments used to silence people and encourage them to self-censor. College campuses are known for their "hate speech" laws, which are very broad and vague. Just wearing a MAGA (make America great again) hat in an unwelcome public place can be considered provocative and get a warning, or even suspension.

Similarly, if you use the wrong pronoun to refer to a person, this can be construed as a micro-aggression and get you tossed from college. As of this writing there are 107 official genders, each with its own pronouns. And it isn't easy to get the right pronoun. Some have taken issue with the forced speech required by using the desired pronouns, and disagreeing with the status quo is also an aggression. Pretty much anyone who disagrees with the cult of victim-hood is punished on a college campus.

Another example of using unofficial punishments is that the UK recently said that they'll refuse to give medical treatment to anyone whom they consider to be a racist or sexist [35]. Included in their definition of racism is anyone who dares to criticize Islam, for example by noting how they treat women like cattle. Note that it's up to any petty bureaucrat to decide if a person is racist or has other undesirable ideas. For example, they could look on your Facebook or do a Google search to see if you ever criticized the government in some way that they consider to be unacceptable.

There is no word yet from Al Gore if he would approve of punishing global warming deniers in this fashion, but it's easy to imagine them extending this policy to cover other disagreeable speech. Then they can pronounce you a bigot or dissident and withhold medical services. No court trial is necessary to take away your rights.

The government will still take a huge amount of money in taxes from the so-called racists, but then will not return it in the form of the promised services. This is especially convenient because those in power can steal medical coverage from someone without having to convict them in a court. The accused will be impoverished by the oppressive taxes, and then get the off-the-books punishment of not being able to get medical care (or even afford their own medical care due to taxation). Those of us in the Western democracies pride ourselves on freedom of expression, but are we really that different from China if undesirable speech can be punished so easily?

It's a laughable mockery of free speech or free thought to consider the current state of rigid orthodoxy on US college campuses. Of course they all give lip service to how they support free speech and value diversity of opinion. But if you happen to have an opinion which differs from the very far left on issues such as global warming, Donald Trump or gender identity, woe to you. You'd be wise to self-censor or you'll likely get thrown out of the university or suspended or at least get much lower grades.

Here's an example from the experience of a family that we knew while my kids were in high school. The boy and girl were both in the same honors English class in high school, and both were very bright kids. The girl would agree with the teacher's political rants on most issues, but the boy would vocally disagree. They would write papers for the class and the girl would consistently get an A while the boy would consistently get a B on his paper. There was no explanation on why the boy's papers were found lacking.

One evening, after writing their papers the two kids had an idea. They would switch the papers, with the boy putting his name on the girl's paper and the girl putting her name on the paper the boy had written. You guessed it: once again the girl got an A and the boy got a B (though his paper had secretly been written by his sister). Obviously, if you want higher grades it's best to agree with all of the political messages espoused by your professors, or at least self-censor and be quiet.

The US public school system has grown weaker every year, with American students scoring at $24^{th}$ place (out of 71 countries) in language, $24^{th}$ in science and a miserable $38^{th}$ place in math compared to the rest of the world [72]. It seems that it's become more important to teach the 107 official genders along with their appropriate pronouns, rather than teaching English and math. Forget about history. Very few schools teach anything more than Martin Luther King. Never mind the Battle of Hastings or the World Wars or the Mayflower Compact. Columbus is strictly out, unless you teach him as the second biggest villain of the past thousand years (behind President Trump of course). The most important things that schools teach are obedience and group think.

Of course they *pretend* to value diversity. In reality, you'll be crushed if you actually have an opinion that differs from that of your teacher. Critical thinking is frowned upon. H.L. Mencken described it well [73]: *"The plain fact is that education is itself a form of propaganda—a deliberate scheme to outfit the pupil, not with the capacity to weigh ideas, but with a simple appetite for gulping ideas ready-made. The aim is to make 'good' citizens, which is to say, docile and uninquisitive citizens.[1]"*

In our coming struggle with China we'll desperately need technological superiority, and American students are particularly weak at science and math. Make no mistake about China's intentions: they do intend for world domination and they are making many of the right moves. They stress practical education in the STEM (science, technology, engineering and math) fields.

Another assault on free speech comes in the form of terrorist groups like ANTIFA. ANTIFA claims to be anti-fascist (hence the name), but if you study their tactics you'll find that they behave very similarly to the actual fascists, such as Mousollini's Blackshirts and Hitler's Brownshirts. For example, they dress all in black, wearing masks so they can't be recognized, and they attack any person or demonstration they consider to be against their beliefs. As a practical matter, they behave like the militant wing of the Democratic Party by attacking Trump supporters as well as genuine fascists like skinheads.

It's also revealing that not one of the 23 Democrats trying for the presidential nomination in 2020 would go on record as condemning ANTIFA [63], even though that group has been listed as a domestic terrorist organization by the US government. That group has been repeatedly shown to attack peaceful protesters [64] they disagree with, as well as beating journalists who would take their pictures or record their illegal actions.

Here is an example of a small way that state and local governments secretly support the ANTIFA terrorist group. In 2017, the right-wing radio host Ben Shapiro and activist Milo Yiannopoulos were scheduled to talk at the University of California Berkeley. ANTIFA opposed any right wing groups being able to speak and caused riots in response.

---

*1. https://www.azquotes.com/quote/417759*

The university and city told the groups they couldn't guarantee their safety and therefore they could no longer speak or hold rallies "at this time". This is a clear violation of free speech using violence, while the local authorities are refusing to do their job and uphold the rights. The Mayor of Seattle has repeated refused to do anything to stop ANTIFA from attacking people or stopping traffic [83].

Consider this thought experiment. A black family wants to buy a house in a formerly white area, but then racists hold rallies and cause riots to prevent it. The authorities tell the black family that they can't guarantee their safety, and therefore they won't be allowed to buy a house here "at this time". Clearly the "at this time" phrase is a kind of weasley way that allows the city to pretend like they care about the rule of law while secretly working to help the racists. People would rightfully be disgusted and say, "Well, the city needs to fight and supply the police to allow the black family to keep their rights." But this dual standard allows the city to support some rights and undermine others.

A decade or two ago, people weren't worried about fake news or about people having a difference of opinion. We had faith that the crazy theories would be demonstrated to be wrong, and that the free and open national discussion would allow us to sort out the truth.

Another problem with our economy and our country is that, before President Trump's tax cuts in 2017, the US had the second highest corporate income tax rates in the world [8], at 39% right behind the UAE. After the tax cuts, the US has a corporate tax rate of about 21%, which is rather in the middle of the pack. You might think that this doesn't affect you, but it does in unseen ways. It's important to remember that the US is competing with other countries around the world in order to attract business and capital.

When corporations are making decisions on which offices to spend more money on and increase staffing levels, they look at total costs.

Tax is often the biggest cost, and so businesses are very sensitive to tax rates. The socialists want to make taxes huge, with the idea that, "They can afford it. Businesses are rich. They'll find a way to pay it." They will indeed find a way to reduce taxes, and one common way is to increase their overseas offices and reduce or close US offices. You never see the jobs that are never created. These statistics are not kept by governments. You only see the results: a sick economy with few jobs created and low wages being paid to workers.

The tax rates paid by different companies vary widely from sector to sector and even between businesses in the same sector. Many large companies like Amazon and Google pay very low taxes [9] because the tax laws have been gamed to help those who know how to play the game. These same large companies contribute a lot of money to political causes, powerful Congressmen and Senators, as well as presidential candidates like Barak Obama and Hillary Clinton [10]. In return, our government officials carefully craft laws to help those businesses on their "friends" list.

An indication of our overall national economic health can be gleaned by looking at how concentrated certain segments are in terms of the percent of business done by one or a few companies. The GAFs (Google-Amazon-Facebook) are the new monopolists, behaving like Standard Oil and the large railroads of the late 19$^{th}$ and early 20$^{th}$ centuries. Except these days almost no one in the US is talking about regulating them, much less breaking them up as had to be done for the large oil and railroad trusts.

In 2012 the world's leading oil company, Exxon, had record profits of $44.9 billion [38]. Democrats were quick to condemn the company and demand in investigation of these unwarranted profits being made "at the expense of the consumer". News reports never mentioned that the oil business is highly cyclical. Oil companies can make a lot of money one year and then have losses the next year.

In 2019, Alphabet (the shell company that owns Google and YouTube) had profits of $46.1 billion [39]. Yet no Democrats or the news media suggested that anything untoward was happening. As mentioned earlier, Google contributes heavily to Democrats and Democratic causes. The connection between political contributions and favorable treatment by the news media or politicians is starting to become clear.

Google and Facebook together take in an amazing 63 percent [11], or nearly 2/3, of all online ad revenue. Similarly, Facebook seems like the only game in town for social media. Amazon controls 49 percent [12] of online retail sales. Clearly having this much control held by these near-monopolies is not equitable for the consumer, yet our politicians and media don't even mention them. In the previous paragraph we looked at how these big companies contribute a lot to the powerful politicians who make the laws. Maybe this has something to do with their special treatment in the US? In Europe, Google has repeatedly been slapped by the courts, but so far the punishments have been mild. Maybe the punishments are tiny and exist just for show as a way to mollify people and get them to shut up about it.

Over time, large institutions become stale and even corrupt. They start to take the attitude that they're the only guardians of truth and order, and anyone challenging their orthodoxy is to be put down harshly. In Japan in the late 1800's, Kanehiro Takaki, surgeon general of the Japanese Imperial Navy, [13] studied why about 25% of Japanese soldiers were sick at any one time from the same malady (throwing up, tingling limbs, and weakness). He found strong evidence to believe that it was due to beriberi (vitamin B1 deficiency).

He proposed to do studies on the navy, giving the men on one ship protein rich meals rather than the traditional diet which was mostly white rice. Both the Navy and their version of the National Institute of Health fought viciously to prevent even the study from taking place. They were so firmly entrenched that these organizations could not allow an outsider to come in and solve such a problem. Takaki eventually won, but it took 20 years to convince the various branches of the military to use the simple cure. This shows how far entrenched bureaucracy will go to protect their turf, regardless of the harm done to the people whom they are purportedly helping.

This same staleness and self-serving characteristic of large institutions can be seen in various US governmental organizations. The FDA (US Food and Drug Administration) [14] effectively serves the purpose of keeping everyone out of the drug business except for the very biggest companies. The average cost to bring a new drug to market, including a long period of testing, is 2.6 billion dollars. This is well out of reach of small and even mid-sized drug companies, and favors Big Pharma by reducing competition. This huge testing cost is passed on to consumers.

The FDA exists supposedly to help make the country healthier by keeping out dangerous and ineffective drugs. However, by making drugs incredibly expensive, they often make good medicines out of reach of many poor and even middle class people. Another problem with this system is that many good medicines are thrown out and never brought to market because it's not economical to pay the mountainous testing costs.

The FDA seems to take the attitude that it's better to keep out 1,000 good medicines rather than allowing one dangerous or ineffective one to be sold. Consider the effect of estrogen-like chemicals on humans: heart disease, diabetes, obesity, reduced fertility. But why does the FDA turn a blind eye to these many problems? The answer is simple: the FDA exists solely to protect the biggest of big business, and plastics are used throughout the food industry.

Meanwhile, in Germany [15] and other European countries, many doctors prescribe herbs and herbal extracts to their patients, showing them to be safe, effective and inexpensive. But in the US no one is willing to pay the high testing costs of an herb or herbal extract. It wouldn't make sound business sense to pay so much to test something that anyone could grow or sell such as milk thistle or chamomile. Since they can't be prescribed, health insurance companies don't like paying for it. These simple and effective treatments are kept out of the hands of Americans in favor of the single molecule type of medicines produced by Big Pharma.

The US pays the highest healthcare costs in the world [16]. Yet our life expectancies are not very good and are even getting worse, as described earlier in this chapter. During the Obama years, the cost of healthcare rose about 50% between the years 2010-2016, or about 7.5% per year. During that time, the official inflation rate published by the US government (see the red line in figure 2, above) averaged only about 2.5% per year. Meaning, healthcare rose at triple the official rate of inflation, even after the celebrated Obamacare. Yet during that same time period the life expectancy went *down*.

If you look closely at the changes in Obamacare, you find that it was mostly a very large transfer of wealth scheme from the middle class to the poor. It was a regressive tax in that the middle class paid a much higher percentage of income than did the rich. Even the Supreme Court had to admit, when they upheld Obamacare in 2012, that it was indeed another large tax increase. The highly liberal news media and websites all like to focus on how costs went down for some, but they ignore how it went up for most of those in the middle. Not only did monthly premiums go up quickly, but the deductible went up to $5,000-$10,000 for a family. This means that you have to pay $10k before the insurance pays anything at all, which is a painful hit for most families and much higher than the old deductibles of $1,000 or $2,000.

While Congress was debating the Obamacare bill, many people were concerned that this new law would mean that their old healthcare plan, which they liked, would have to close. In order to diffuse this criticism, President Obama repeatedly said [77], "If you like your healthcare plan, you can keep it." This was shown to be a blatant lie when most of the old healthcare plans were forced to close or had to charge much higher premiums in order to be able to cover those that they would lose money on.

It was a way to force the middle class to subsidize the poor. Yes, you can keep your healthcare plan, but now you have to pay double for it. H.L. Mencken gave a good description of just this sort of situation: "*The men the American people admire most extravagantly are the most daring liars; the men they detest most violently are those who try to tell them the truth.*" But in this case, Obama's lie was a good political expedient that pacified the people enough to get the law passed.

Public schools in the US spend the most per student in the world [17], yet our students are only ranked 38$^{th}$ place (out of 71 countries) in math, 24$^{th}$ in science and 24th in language skills [18]. Year after year, the US has been steadily declining in terms of how well educated our students are. Yes, they can recite all of the great things (but none of the negatives) about the identity politics heroes like Martin Luther King, Harvey Milk, Hillary Clinton, Cesar Chavez and Malcolm X. They know all of the 107 official genders as well as the alphabet song, but know nothing about the history of Western civilization, the US Constitution or WWII (except that Hitler was the bad guy, and that Trump is exactly like Hitler). Is it any wonder that other countries continue to pull ahead of the US since our students are so poorly educated?

The justice system and penal system in the US is failing us too. The United States has among the highest incarceration rates in the world, with 0.7 percent of our population in jail/prison [19]. This doesn't include the millions more who are on probation or parole. And the US spends the most per prisoner in the world [20a]. With this huge expense in number of prisoners and amount spent per prisoner, we still get very poor performance with our penal system, showing a recidivism rate of 68% (number of prisoners re-arrested within 3 years) [20b].

One disgusting and shocking trend in the US is the rise of private prisons. Initially, these were attractive to politicians because they could pass a law to use private prisons and not have to ask the voters for permission to build a prison, by way of a bond issue. Whenever possible, politicians will always choose the no-accountability option of not letting the unwashed masses decide what the politicians can do with money that is rightfully the property of the political class.

That's how our masters in government view it: that the money is rightfully theirs so they shouldn't have to seek permission from the little people. Notice that in either case (a bond issue or private prison) the people will need to pay a stream of future money, in the form of taxes, to either the bondholders or the private prison owners.

However, studies have shown that the private prisons [21b] are more expensive over time. The private prisons usually have a contract whereby the government promises to keep a certain percentage of the prison filled. If there are too few prisoners, then the government is penalized and must pay extra money. So this creates a system whereby the government no longer has the ideal situation being where there are very few prisoners, but now the ideal situation is to have as many prisoners as possible! Every prisoner is a source of profit.

Private prisons take the approach that they have captive customers (quite literally) and can therefore charge a high price for everything. These prisons consult dietitians who advise them on the average calorie needs of a person, and then they give the prisoners just barely this amount. Note that the prisons ignore the dietitians when they advise that a balanced diet should include a certain amount of fruits and vegetables as well as meat or other protein source like beans. Instead, prisoners are fed a lot of carbohydrate and fat-rich foods because these are the cheapest on a per-calorie basis.

Many of the prisoners are near starvation, but this is by design. The prison commissary sells other foods but at hugely marked up prices, such as $4 for a pack of ramen noodles that would cost 20 cents in the grocery [22]. Food becomes the medium of exchange between prisoners. You don't want to get beat up or stabbed? Then you'll need to pay 4 packs of ramen a week to your cell block gang leader.

Prisoners are forced to beg family and friends to deposit money into their commissary accounts so they can afford the extra food. In order to make this system work, it must be strictly illegal to allow friends or family to give food—even canned food or tamper-proof packages—to the prisoners, for fear that it will undercut the commissary prices. But don't worry; there is always some good excuse for not allowing someone to have food brought in. You can say that outside food could be laced with drugs or carry diseases. Any excuse suits a tyrant, or a tyrannical system.

Everything else about the private prison is also considered to be a profit center and is operated at hugely marked up prices. You want to make a phone call? That's $2 a minute subtracted from your commissary account. You want to use the internet? That's $2 a minute. You have a cough and can't get to sleep? Well that's not nearly serious enough for a visit to the infirmary, but don't worry because the commissary will sell you a box of cough drops for only $7.

I can hear many people saying, "Well, it serves them right. They committed crimes so now they have to suffer for it." To an extent that's true. But consider that many people in jail or prison, perhaps most of them, are there for non-violent offenses such as possession of drugs, tax evasion, or minor theft. Do we really want to take these people and convert them from otherwise productive people who help the economy and pay taxes, into psychopaths who just want to cause as much pain and suffering upon a society that inflicted huge misery on them?

About a hundred years ago, Clyde Barrow was locked up for auto theft because he was late in returning a rental car, while still in his teens. While in prison he was repeatedly raped by an older and stronger inmate, and he eventually bashed in the guy's head with a rock. This had the effect of making Clyde hate all of society and consider it profoundly immoral and unfair. Perhaps his conclusion was partly right. The net effect was that Bonnie and Clyde went on a long killing spree before they themselves were gunned down in 1934. So before you work too hard to emphasize punishment over rehabilitation, consider the long-term results. Do you want to create psychopaths? Because that's how you create psychopaths.

I'm not at all some bleeding-heart liberal who says that we should hug and coddle prison inmates while making their cells filled with decorative hearts and Hello Kitty posters. Rather, perhaps we need to look at other countries that have far fewer people in prison and far lower recidivism rates, and try to learn some things to make our prisons better. And don't worry, being locked up and not being able to go where you want or see your wife or girlfriend for years is already a lot of punishment. But blindly emphasizing more and more punishment, with no compassion nor having any hope that someone will reintegrate to society, is a recipe for more crime. Private prison companies make a lot of money by perpetuating this system, but it does a lot of harm to society.

The big private prison companies like CCA pay a lot of money to political parties [23], state and federal, in order to keep the money flowing in and to keep as many prisoners as possible for as long as possible. And if prisoners can't find jobs because of their new prison record, then that's great because many of them will commit theft, burglary or drug trafficking and be back into the prison system. Cha-ching! It's all good. Well, maybe it's not so good for society, or the prisoners or their families, but it's good for the bottom line of CCA and it's good to generate more political contributions. The people who really matter (the aristocracy in DC) consider it a win-win situation.

In this chapter I've tried to show some areas where the US has gotten worse over time, and how we're still getting worse. I've shown how the federal and state governments cheat at the statistics to make things look better than they are. Now let's look at why things went downhill and why they're likely to keep getting even worse.

# Chapter 2:
# Contributing Factors and Causes

———

BEFORE WE EXAMINE THE true causes of the decline, let's consider the usual list of false causes that the media repeats endlessly.

# False causes given for the decline:

———

**THE OPIOID CRISIS**: It's true that more people have been dying of drug overdoses in recent years, for example with fentanyl made in China, but this is more of a symptom than a cause, as was described in the previous chapter. When people are faced with a grim and desperate reality, many of them will try to cover up their problems and numb their minds with drugs and alcohol. To see through this excuse, just recall that this country has had access to alcohol, crack cocaine, heroin, methamphetamines, and other drugs for centuries. Why, suddenly, should so many people be turning to these drugs?

Edgar Allen Poe was plagued by his own addictions to opium and alcohol and said this [68]: "*I have absolutely no pleasure in the stimulants in which I sometimes so madly indulge. It has not been in the pursuit of pleasure that I have periled life and reputation and reason. It has been the desperate attempt to escape from the torturing memories, from a sense of insupportable loneliness and a dread of some strange impending doom.*" For Poe, and millions of others, the addictions are just a symptom of deep unhappiness and an attempt to escape it, even for a short while.

I believe that people are now trying more to escape the misery brought on by an economy being destroyed and taking down the middle class who have worked so hard to build up their modest lives. When Russia went through their smaller collapse in the early 1990's, millions of people there turned to the traditional Russian escape of vodka, and during that period alcoholism soared. Again, vodka wasn't the cause of their downfall, but a symptom of the people's misery.

**Global warming**: This is the bogeyman our politicians and media love to blame for everything. No doubt they'll try to blame the reduced standard of living on global warming. This book isn't meant to argue that issue, but simply consider this: The wealthy and their puppets, (e.g. actors), are always warning about global warming and enormous rises in the sea level. And yet they continue to buy ocean-front property. In fact, the price of ocean front property is near all-time highs. It seems that if they actually believed their own hype they wouldn't waste money on a house that will be underwater in a year or two.

If you only pay attention to the negatives of global warming, then you're led to believe that we'll have much lower crop yields, thus driving up the cost of food. But if one strip of land at a certain latitude is too warm, then a strip at a higher latitude—such as Canada and Siberia—now has warmer and longer growing seasons than before, increasing yield. The increased carbon dioxide in the atmosphere can also contribute to greater crop yields everywhere because it causes plants to grow faster. These positive relationships are always ignored in the global warming hype.

The great theoretical physicist Freeman Dyson has criticized [55] the global warming hysteria saying that it was "grossly exaggerated". He noted that those pushing the agenda ignore the positive effects such as some areas of the world getting improved crop yields. He has also pointed out that the simulations aren't reliable and was one of the signatories of the World Climate Declaration denying that there exists a global warming emergency. You never hear about him and many other brilliant minds simply because they disagree with the hegemony that has been imposed on academia by Western governments. We hear all about the wonderful computer models predicting global warming, but when the predictions turn out to be wrong then the billionaire-controlled media ignores it. Back in the early 1970's there was a big global cooling hysteria where many people (and computer models) predicted a coming ice age.

Some, like Al Gore, even go so far as to suggest that we should punish the global warming deniers [56] like Dyson above. Punishing people for an opposing viewpoint is not the mark of science, but is actually close to the behavior of a barbaric sort of religion. Dyson wasn't at all a conservative, but identified himself as a liberal, having voted for President Obama and opposed the Vietnam War. Most of those selling the global warming hysteria claim that everyone who opposes it are reactionary conservatives. They resort to this sort of ad hominem arguments because their movement is more like religion and less like science, though of course they wrap themselves in science and claim to be very thorough.

When you read the global warming articles in the billionaire-controlled media, you get the idea that it's perfectly understood and that it is "settled science" as the self-proclaimed experts tell it. But then you find out that they claim that the global warming theories support contradictory results.

A few years ago, the water levels in the Great Lakes were well below average [67]. Many articles appeared saying that this was exactly what was predicted by the global warming theories. But then a few years later, the water levels were much higher than normal, and again the global warming theories said that this proved that they were right. But if a theory is proved right by collecting data showing that something is moving up, and is also proved right by it moving down, then there is no conceivable way to collect any possible data that could disprove the theory. The ideas that are completely disconnected from facts are religion, not science.

I bring up global warming not to try to disprove the theories in this small space. Global warming is just a convenient whipping boy for me to complain about the larger problem of politicizing science. I'm pointing out how people are disgusted by the experts talking out of both sides of their mouth and claiming that it's good science. This has a corrosive effect on the public, and leads to a distrust of all science. Then we get people who believe that vaccines cause autism and distrust other scientific findings, which is very unfortunate. We shouldn't politicize science because it leads to these serious problems.

**Greedy corporations**: Of course they're greedy. We all want the most we can get for any products or services that we have to offer. In fact, you might even say that corporations have a fiducial duty to be greedy since they're required by law to do whatever they judge to maximize shareholder value, subject to the constraints of the law, ethics, risk aversion and the laws of physics. Corporations are no more greedy now than they were 20 or even 100 years ago. Perhaps companies are more often allowed to go off on greedy and anti-social directions now because corrupt politicians look the other way and refuse to enforce the anti-trust laws, for example against the GAFs (Google-Amazon-Facebook).

**Failure of capitalism**: Those who push for more government control over people and the economy love to use the excuse that everything harmful is due to the failure of capitalism. But they ignore the past 200 years of history which has shown time and time again that capitalistic countries grew and were prosperous, lifting millions out of misery and poverty. While countries that went to government control often went from riches to rags. Read about what harm came to Cuba in the 1960's, Venezuela and Argentina in the 2000's, Bolivia and others. If you look closely at the supposed failures of capitalism, you find that the failures (to create jobs, lift people from poverty, etc.) were due to over-regulation, over-taxation and cronyism. It's free-market capitalism that has helped people and it's blind government control that has destroyed people's ability to create wealth.

Many politicians point to big corporations leaving the US and taking their jobs with them. But this is mistaking the symptom for the cause. Corporations and capital will leave the US (as they came to the US in the past 150 years) not due to greed or charity, but rather because it is the best choice for optimizing their return. Corporations have left the US because the US has become inhospitable to the "rich". Politicians on the left, and increasingly on the right, attack the corporations and rich investors. This drives out capital, and in turn kills jobs. There's more detail about this later in this chapter, under Actual Causes.

**Racism**: Many left-wing politicians and their allies in the media and academia always love to bring up racism. They say that corporations are trying to hurt people just because they hate many other races. This is silly. Corporations merely want to make more money, and as pointed out above they're legally required to try to make more money. They hire and promote minorities because it's a good business decision, not because they're forced by law.

Increasingly, we're seeing politicians talk about paying enormous reparations for slavery. This plays well to many black people who want another big handout from the government. But the plan has so many problems. You can't find the supposed slave owners or even their descendants because they died over 100 years ago and many generations have passed. If one of your great-great-great-grandparents owned slaves, are you responsible for a $1/32^{nd}$ share of reparations? The calculations become impossible.

There are similar problems in finding the victims. Clearly, the actual victims are long dead, but how do we identify their offspring? Maybe some would suggest doing DNA testing and finding a person's percentage of African ancestry. But many people came to the US from Africa (via Haiti, Cuba, etc.) after slavery was abolished. You can't identify the evildoers or the victims. And what about white people who were victimized by these same aristocracy who abused the slaves? Shouldn't the white victims' descendants also be compensated? Again, you can't find the victims or the perpetrators.

**Sexism**: This is just another red herring brought up by politicians to try to divide society and get people to vote for them. There's no good reason to believe that the drop in the US standard of living is by some group of people trying to push down women.

**Other identity politics**: Again, like racism and sexism above, there are no good reasons to think that some evildoers are destroying the US economy because they hate LGBTQ+ or other groups. It's merely a hot-button issue that gets a few more people to buy into blaming the wrong people for our current (and accelerating) problems without having to think too much.

# Actual causes of the decline:

———

**GOVERNMENT CONTROL and over-regulation:** Almost every year, the US piles more and more regulations on various companies. Transportation (FAA), drugs (the FDA), the internet and all aspects of our lives continue to be over-regulated. And yet the FAA is so blinded that they can't prevent the fiasco of approving the 737 MAX system, even though pilots had complained that the system malfunctioned and was dangerous. The big regulatory bodies are in bed with the giant companies (Boeing, Merck, Pfizer, Johnson&Johnson, etc.), and only work to protect profits rather than protecting the consumer.

**High taxes:** Taxes continue to increase throughout the economy. Government produces nothing of value, but only moves around goods and services produced by others (inefficiently and counter-productively). Yet it's a fun way to pass time for the political aristocracy, and so they find ways to increase taxes every year. Okay, to be fair, Trump reduced taxes on the middle-class with his 2017 tax cuts, but that was an anomaly, more of a hiccup in the overall trend.

The many hours spent calculating your taxes and then having to pay them would be bad enough, but economists tend to agree that taxes have the effect to slow overall economic growth, meaning that it gets harder for people to find jobs and those jobs tend to pay less.

**Out of control spending and unsustainable debt levels:** In Chapter 1 we looked at how the national debt is growing faster than the economy and therefore faster than the US government's ability to pay the interest. Most economists agree that unlimited government borrowing and debt have a depressing and slowing effect on the economy. It only makes sense: if the government is borrowing enormous amounts of money in the credit markets, then there's less money for private business to borrow. Therefore businesses have a harder time expanding, so fewer jobs are created and pay increases are reduced.

**Breakdown in the rule of law:** The rule of law means that there are written laws, rules and procedures, and that those are followed by the courts without any differences between how people are treated. That's why you see the statues of Justice personified as a woman blindfolded with a sword and scale. The scale means that she only weighs the facts. The blindfold means that she doesn't care who it is. Of course, with any system that requires honesty, there is a continuum of points to compare from the very corrupt to the squeaky clean. Maybe China with its rampant cronyism is on one end of the scale and Switzerland is on the other end. But I think that if you're honest about your analysis, you'll find that we in the US have been moving steadily toward the "China" side. Transparency International [89] listed the US at a corruption rank of 23 (lower is least corrupt) in 2019, falling from their rank of 18 in 2016.

One example from recent history occurred in 2016 when the country learned that Hillary Clinton had kept a secret email server and transferred many hundreds, perhaps thousands, of secret and top-secret documents to this server. Of course, it's strictly against government rules and she had to know that, having worked in government for decades. Due to her intentionally ignoring the rules, WikiLeaks, Russia and China got access to many documents. James Comey and the FBI did their investigation and said that it wasn't intentional. But setting up the secret server was intentionally. Transferring documents out of their safe government protected system onto her weak and unprotected system were both intentional.

I personally worked for over 30 years as an engineer doing missile guidance and autopilot work for the biggest defense companies. You would certainly recognize the names. All during that time I was required to have a security clearance. Along with any security clearance, every year you have mandatory training where they remind you, again and again, that you have a solemn duty to protect national secrets, and they spell out for you exactly what you are and are not permitted to do. You can't transfer any documents from a secure system to an unsecure one (such as your personal laptop or home computer). If I transferred one document to myself in email, for example, and that document went to my personal laptop I could and would be prosecuted.

But Hillary Clinton did this hundreds of times and she wasn't prosecuted. It was her intentional disregard for the rules that caused these documents to fall into enemy hands. Okay, the American people did see fit to make her lose the presidency to Donald Trump, which is a small amount of justice, but what about the damage to national security? This is an obvious example of how the justice system depends on who you are.

If you read the Bill of Rights in the US Constitution, you find (Fifth Amendment) that there are rules regarding when the government is allowed to take your property or lock you in prison. This is often called due process and has been more carefully defined over time as courts have filled in the various details. The summary of this law is that the government is required to give you a fair trial before locking you up or fining you. But in the past 20 years this rule has been gutted by the Bush-Obama administrations purportedly to help the drug war. If you have money and are suspected of drugs or other illegal activity, then police can simply take it. They're not required to press charges against you at all. It's up to you to take them to court and try to get your money back.

There have been many documented cases where people were carrying a few thousand dollars with the intent of buying a car. The police found the cash and took it. The people might be able to hire an attorney, but it would cost them perhaps $10,000 to recover $3,000. And there's no guarantee that the individual would win, since it's often very difficult to prove that you're *not* a drug dealer. Of course the police are aware of this, which is why they have a big incentive to steal any cash that they find.

Other recent developments that obviously violate the due process clause are the so-called "red line" laws. Basically, these laws make it very easy for police to steal any guns that you have just based on some hearsay evidence that someone is "concerned" about your mental health. There isn't required any sort of investigation much less a trial. They don't have a psychologist question you or any other real fact gathering. The police simply take your guns. And again, it's up to you to somehow try to prove that you're innocent, which is often very difficult. You can hire an attorney and spend many thousands of dollars, just as if they stole your property, and again you might very well win, but in the end you spent far more than the guns were worth. Liberals love this law because anything that helps to disarm the population and get rid of guns (except in police hands) is viewed as desirable.

A related repellent law is the one where anyone who is simply accused of domestic violence (but without any trial or conviction) can lose their guns or have a restraining order created which prevents them from even sleeping in their own home. The Constitution is supposed to protect people from being punished based on some unfounded accusation. Keep in mind that domestic violence can be something as simple as slapping someone. If you get in an argument with a stranger and slap them, yes you can be fined or even put in jail for a few days for assault. But it's a misdemeanor and is recognized as being a rather low-level crime.

I'm not justifying domestic abuse, and I'm quite sure that those who attack this book will say that I'm arguing in favor of men beating women to death. Those are horrible crimes, and they're already felonies. I'm merely asking to try to keep a bit of perspective, not to go to extremes, and to retain due process of law. One doesn't even have to be accused of any felony and the victim doesn't have to show any real injuries, but merely to allege that the gun owner slapped them or is mentally unstable. Some wives game this system and use it to punish their husbands for something as simple as a purely verbal domestic squabble.

Here's a common trick used by those who are arguing for more government control or reducing individual rights incrementally more. They find the most horrible example they can, for example the domestic abuse case mentioned above with a man beating a woman to death. Then they craft a law that will cover that case, and vastly more. But they only argue it for that one case, and don't bother justifying that the law can quite easily be used on very minor cases to exact enormous punishment.

Using the ill-founded law, prosecutors can charge someone who did something minor with a law that has draconian punishments, and then plea bargain them to plead guilty to something that's still way too much. People don't want to go to jail for 20 years, so they plea bargain for 5 years for something minor.

Part of the rule of law requires that the laws be written down and are applied evenly to everyone. There are two ways of considering the law, de jure and de facto law. De jure law means the law exactly as it is written. De facto law means the law as it really is. In places and times when the rule of law is strongly followed, then de jure law is the same as de facto law. In increasingly corrupt regimes, there become huge differences between what is written and how the law is actually applied.

In the US, consider the usage of the N-word. I'm not even allowed to write the word because that will cause my book to be thrown out of Amazon and also I'd likely lose my YouTube and email accounts. This also brings up part of the reason why Amazon and Google (owner of YouTube) need to be broken up: the ability of monopolies to inflict extra judicial punishments, as we'll cover later in Chapter 5.

Back to the discussion about the N-word. The written law (de jure) in the First Amendment to the Constitution says that you have complete free speech, except for a few narrow cases such as fraud, libel or inciting violence. But in reality, the usage of the N-word is poorly defined, which is not an indication of a system where the rule of law is strong. Black people are allowed to use the word but white people aren't, is the simple way of stating the law.

Part of the problem is that you can't separate people and say that certain rules apply to one group and not another. A second part of the problem is just how to define a black person. If you're accused of racism you can lose your job instantly, no trial necessary. However a recognized defense is to say that you are black and are therefore allowed to use the term.

But how do we define black? If a DNA test shows that you have 70% African heritage, does this make it legal? How about 50% (like President Obama) or 30%? We need a cutoff line, but it isn't defined anywhere, and therefore the law is not properly defined. However, the punishments for being a convicted racist are very real: loss of job, kicked out of university, loss of internet accounts and extreme public shaming.

Also, according to the Fourth Amendment, the government is not allowed to do searches and seizures of your house or *papers* unless they get a warrant. I emphasize papers here because it isn't very much of a stretch to include computer files along with your papers. After all, we use computers to keep track of all our personal information these days exactly as people used paper, or parchment 200 years ago. Yet since 9/ 11 the government has worked tirelessly to squash down any sort of privacy rights.

When Edward Snowden revealed the shocking levels of abuse by the NSA of spying on American citizens, President Obama promised [49] to reform the NSA. But those promises lacked any sort of transparency. They were merely meant to get the public to breathe a sigh of relief that it was "all taken care of". There was never anyone impartial who was put in charge of verifying that the reforms were implemented. The Obama promise was cynically made with no intention of ever carrying it out, just waiting for it all to blow over.

And did it blow over? The NSA (using the telecoms as the foil) today collects even more data on every single person in the US and records every call you make. They force your internet provider to record every single website you ever visit. Your phone has GPS and sends that position information to Google, so they know (and are required to provide to the NSA, FBI or any other government agency) every single place you have ever visited and the precise times you were there.

Obama did sign the deceptively named USA Freedom Act [50], but this did nothing at all to restore privacy. It moved the storage of all your phone calls to telecom companies rather than the NSA. Note that the NSA can still get instant access to the phone calls because the telecom companies are required to give any data to the NSA and other law enforcement agencies. But the telecom companies and Google are subject to gag rules and are forbidden to tell the public or the media about all of the warrantless searches performed by the spy agencies. By moving it to the telecom companies, all that this really did is to make it cheaper for the NSA and more expensive for telecom companies, and thus another hidden tax was created and passed along to the consumer.

And what does the NSA do with all of this data? It's cloaked in secrecy with no public auditor. Can a right wing president use the NSA to gain access to the comings and goings of left-wing journalists in order to find and jail any leakers? Maybe the data is sometimes used to discredit journalists and political challengers by covertly revealing embarrassing details to other press members? How many times have they spied on you because you are connected, through several degrees of separation, to some suspected whistle-blower?

**Factionalization:** *"Years of love have been forgotten in a minute of hatred."* - Edgar Allen Poe. It's no accident that politicians like to break us up into factions and then encourage the factions to fear, and ultimately to hate, each other. Those on the left fear that the right will outlaw all abortions, while those on the right fear that a liberal government will outlaw all guns, leaving them defenseless against criminals. Maybe it's time for a true centrist who will promise to make no changes to existing abortion laws or existing gun regulation.

Instead, both the Republicans and Democrats become increasingly radicalized with each passing year. Thirty or forty years ago, Republicans and Democrats could have sensible conversations on policy and the direction of the country, but that's impossible now. Both sides are now filled with demagogues who only stir hatred rather than thought. Paul Craig Roberts put it well when he said: *"As the growing emphasis on feelings crowds out reason, facts will play a smaller role in public discourse."*

**Acceptance of corruption:** Many people have lost faith in the institutions in the United States. Universities researchers are caught fudging numbers to make global warming look worse [45] than it actually is. Government workers in the FBI are caught spying on Trump [46] during the 2016 election to try to help Clinton. The SPLC (Southern Poverty Law Center) is caught abusing minorities [47], sexually abusing women and having almost no diversity in its nearly all-white staff. The list goes on, and it's easy to grow cynical from all of the revealed corruption.

Eventually, people take the attitude that they just don't care if one of their elected officials is caught accepting bribes (like the Clinton Foundation did [48]). The attitude becomes "at least he/she is on our side". People expect that the other side is corrupt and so they tolerate unlimited corruption from the people on their own side. This acceptance of open corruption is typical of other empires in decline too, as during the decline of the Roman and Spanish empires.

**Corruption of Academia:** In academia, the professors who get promoted, for example to department chair, are the ones who publish the most papers and the ones who bring in the most money in research grants. The US government is the biggest source of funding for research grants. But the grant money comes with strings. In order to get further phases of the grant, you need to pass review by government officials. The easiest way to pass review is to give the answer they want to hear.

For example, with regard to global warming, it's a much easier path for you to find some new way to support the global warming narrative than to challenge it, even if you have good data. The researchers are under so much pressure to bring in more grant money that they've even been caught manufacturing data [45] or ignoring data that didn't fit the desired narrative.

From 2016-2018 the global temperatures measured by NASA actually went down, which put into doubt the global warming panic. They came under such intense political pressure that they were forced to change their methodology [53] in order to compute the data differently and therefore get the desired answer that temperatures went up during that time. The scientists who work and profit in the global warming hysteria industry seem to follow the creed from the song "*In the Garden of Allah*" by Don Henley [71]:

"*I can get you any result you like.*

*What's it worth to you?*

*Because there is no wrong.*

*There is no right.*

*And I sleep very well at night.*"

Another example of academics cynically doing anything for politicians is how those espousing MMT (modern monetary theory) justify boundless deficits and money printing. MMT is essentially a rehashing of Keynesianism, which is the idea that the government should print tons of money to stimulate the economy. Printing tons of money is a way to steal from savers, and theft has a long and rich tradition in government. Global warming and MMT are both very desirable to those who want ever-increasing control of the economy, and so these academics are rewarded with research grants.

The corruption of academia can be viewed in terms of "*Attila and the Witch Doctor*" which Ayn Rand put forth over 50 years ago [52]. The Attila is a person who has a lot of power but little understanding or sophistication, like a warlord or politician. The witch doctor is someone who is intelligent and can come up with long and complex treatises on how and why things happen, but they're very weak physically. The witch doctor was typically someone like a mystic, priest or philosopher, but in more modern times academics have stepped in to fill the demand.

Attila and the witch doctor need each other. Attila needs someone to justify him, to excuse his awful behavior to the masses. The witch doctor is the self-proclaimed "expert" who can con the masses and get them to accept, trust and follow Attila. During feudal times, the witch doctor would come up with theories like the divine right of kings, that they are simply chosen by God to rule. And no one can question the priest because he has immense authority and the mighty Church to fall back on. The witch doctor needs Attila because, left to his own devices, the witch doctor has no abilities in the real world. The witch doctor needs to be protected and fed because he is so inept at basic real world skills. In our modern world, Attila represents those in government who have the power. The witch doctor represents the academics who can come up with justifications for anything that Attila wants to do.

**News media concentration:** In the past 20 years, the news media have gradually become more and more concentrated in a few hands. Rather than having any competition in ideas, they all converge toward representing the interests of their billionaire owners.

**The Social Security nightmare:** This was a Ponzi scheme from the start. It only worked for as long as it did (80 years) because of the growing population and time that it took for people to grow old and start claiming benefits. But now the native population isn't growing. Birthrates in the US are near all-time lows [26]. While it's true that the US population is growing, that's almost entirely due to immigration from Mexico. But these new immigrants are mostly a lot of poor people (as most new immigrants have been for hundreds of years) who pay very little into the Social Security system, while many higher paid workers are retiring every day and expecting large SS checks in their retirement.

Clearly the system will need sizable tax increases or benefit cuts; most likely we will see one or both of these. We'll look at more detail on how this is going to be affected in Chapter 3. At this point, just be aware that Social Security, along with Medicare/Medicaid, together make up 48% [44] of government spending already, and it gets worse each year. The spending increases are locked in because SS has a cost of living adjustment each year. Congress is the only one with the power to pass new laws and fix the mess, but they have no incentive to do so. Therefore it will continue to get worse, pushing the US toward the debt cliff.

**Representation without taxation:** In the American Revolution, the people were understandably aggrieved by the British parliament continually increasing their tax levels, even though the American Colonies didn't have any representation in the parliament. "No taxation without representation" was the rallying cry. Naturally, the parliament was generous with tax increases because it is always fun for politicians to liberally use OPM (other people's money), just as our masters in Washington now use our money. One ruling aristocracy has been replaced with a new one, nothing more.

Today we have what at first glance might seem to be the opposite situation of representation without taxation, but curiously it leads to the same situation as taxation without representation. Many millions of people can vote and elect candidates, but these people are immune to the federal income tax because the tax tables and deductions are set high enough to ignore all of the low income earners.

In the US, nearly 76 million people [31], or 44 percent of the US electorate, pay no income tax. Many people criticize this analysis by saying "Ah but they pay sales tax!" That is true, but sales taxes are quite a bit smaller than income tax. And when we're talking about the wasteful spending at the federal level, that is funded mostly by income taxes on individuals and businesses.

Since so many people don't have to pay income tax, they're naturally in favor of increasing almost any federal programs. After all, everything is paid for by someone else. If you could vote to tax people who lived in a galaxy far away and you got lots of free goodies as a result, would you be happy to get it? Politicians can count on millions of people giving a resounding "Yes, please!" to that question. And so taxes increase every year, which slows the economy, kills the creation of new jobs and furthers the hollowing-out process of the middle class.

**Fighting endless wars:** The US has been fighting wars with most of the world's population in recent years, and this is just a partial list: We're fighting a proxy war with Russia in Syria, as well as sanctions on Russia and various members of their leadership. We have an enormous trade war with China, affecting hundreds of billions of dollars in business. Also with China, we have been waging a mostly unsuccessful diplomatic war to discourage their claiming vast territories of the South China Sea. The Chinese build new islands by dredging up a lot of sand and rocks, then saying that the island is Chinese, even though it's within the territorial waters of the Philippines, Vietnam or Indonesia. It's a power grab and the US has done badly in their efforts to build any consensus against it.

We're also in a pointless trade war with the European Union over subsidies for aircraft and some other issues. Then there are the 40-60 year old sanctions against Iran and Cuba, plus a few proxy wars against Iran in Lebanon and Yemen. And who could forget the bitter little tyrant in North Korea who sets off a nuclear weapon or launches a missile over Japan whenever he feels that he's not getting enough international attention.

The Roman Empire (among others) also had many wars along their vast frontiers in their waning years. These constant little wars sapped the strength, manpower, will to fight and treasure of that empire and it's happening right now to the US as well. The US really needs to make peace with many of these, even if means giving up a little to each of our opponents. Trying to fight everyone at once is obviously a losing game.

A careful, organized retreat can save an uncontrolled and catastrophic collapse later. Let France and Germany keep subsidizing Airbus. We can make a deal with them and have Europe in our corner again as we did during the cold war. Ignore North Korea until they do something like sinking another ship, then sink one of their slightly larger ships. Let Russia keep Syria and maybe even half of Ukraine while we pull back some of the missile stationed in Poland and their other Eastern European satellites, but enlist their help in pressuring Iran to actually stopping their nuclear arms program.

Currently Iran always promises to stop the nuclear work, and then Obama or someone gets a big prize and weeks of fawning press coverage for achieving "peace in our time" [80]. Later, we find out that the latest deal was worthless because it had no significant provision for inspectors to verify that nuclear work was halted. But Russia can help with that. Russia has almost as much incentive to stop a nuclear Iran as the US does, since Iran is on their doorstep.

The big stumbling block to peace with Russia is that the Democratic party will attack any and all peace overtures as proving that Trump is a Russian mole. They keep pushing this completely fact-free narrative over and over so that many people think that it's true. The Mueller Report showed that that whole thing was a "big fat nothingburger", yet the implications persist. In this way, the Democratic Party keeps the US in a worthless power struggle with Russia.

I am no fan of Russia and grew up during the cold war which we feared could be turned into a hot war very quickly. I read the Solzhenitsyn books like "*A Day in the Life of Ivan Denisovich*", hating their human rights abuses and their communist ideology for decades. But we need to make a deal with Russia in order to put our efforts into the one struggle that really matters: China.

The real existential struggle that the US faces now is with China. Keep in mind that Russia's economy is only about one quarter as large as China. Military might comes from economic power, and China continues to build more military hardware and modernize much more quickly than does Russia. Yes, Russia has nuclear weapons but the rest of their military is not a serious threat. There should be no doubt that China is our really big threat, and their threat is projected to grow since their economy is growing around 6% per year while the American economy grows at best 2-3%.

The reason that no one wants to talk about the Chinese problem is twofold. First, both Democrat and Republican billionaire's have large investments in China. Second, Hillary and other Democrats accepted large donations from several people with close ties to the Chinese Communist Party (CCP), [81], [82]. They need to keep people focused on Russia so that everyone ignores the real threat of the Chinese. They're so desperate and hungry for power that they accept that it hurts our country, as long as it helps them to gain power.

China invented gunpowder around 900 years ago, but they did very little with it aside form fireworks and entertainment. The Europeans used the gunpowder to make cannons, which had an unprecedented effect on war. Before the cannon, castles reigned supreme. A castle stood as a large and easily visible symbol of a kingdom's strength and power.

But by the end of the 1400's cannons could easily defeat castles, making them a death trap for those caught inside the crumbling walls. Cannon balls travel much farther than arrows, so an army could lay siege to a castle from great distance and eventually reduce the castle to rubble while the attacker suffered very little damage.

Some countries continued to put their resources into castles. Other countries wisely put their defense spending into cannons, and the latter ultimately dominated. This is the position that the US is in right now, spending money on large and showy, but vulnerable, aircraft carriers. I'm not suggesting that we reduce defense spending, but rather that we reallocate our defense spending to more efficient areas.

China has been quietly putting a lot of their defense spending into pulling ahead of the US in three key areas. A breakthrough in any one area would give them the kind of advantage that the US had at the end of WWII by being the only nuclear power. The difference is that the Chinese are not shy about using force and would likely use it on us very quickly, to decisive effect. And we can't count on them to be benevolent masters. The areas in which Chinese have been building up their capability are quantum applications, AI (artificial intelligence) and hypersonic vehicles. Many books have been written on the workings and impact of these technologies, but I'll keep it short here.

Quantum applications include both quantum computing and quantum tunneling. Quantum computing is a new way of computing that could be thousands or millions of times faster than our conventional computers. This would give the Chinese the ability to break many of our codes rapidly. Missiles are often somewhat autonomous, but they can still be redirected from the ground by way of coded transmissions. The impact of having no workable codes would be devastating.

Aside from knowing exactly what we were going to do, it also would allow them to break into our drones or missiles and make those self-destruct, or worse turn them against us. That isn't science fiction. Fortunately, it isn't science fact just yet either, but our researchers still don't know if it's possible nor how quantum computers could be made in a cost effective way. So far only a few small qubits (quantum bits) have been made and it would be very expensive to make a large computer using present methods.

Quantum tunneling is a somewhat related technology that allows someone to separate a pair of linked particles. Then if one particle is changed that influences the other particle from a distance, allowing completely secure communications that can't be broken without the sender and designated receiver being made aware. The Chinese claim to have created a quantum communication network between Beijing and Shanghai, though this hasn't been completely verified [78], [79].

Artificial intelligence is the second area in which China is pouring vast amounts of research money [74] and could be used to threaten the US in important and unforeseen ways. Artificial intelligence refers to making computers that can mimic a brain, either with software or specialized hardware or both. Many smart people, such as Elon Musk and Stephen Hawking, have warned about creating AI because once it becomes much more intelligent than humans then it will have its own motives and plans. Because the AI can out-think humans it might decide that humans are unnecessary and create wars or viruses to kill us, much like Skynet in the Terminator movies.

But well before AI becomes super intelligent, it can still be very useful to sift through data and find nuclear submarines, predict how an opponent will conduct a war, create the most effective propaganda or even take steps to undermine a foreign economy. The possible applications are vast and infinitely varied, so it's difficult to imagine all the things that could be done with AI. One danger is that some country or group could achieve a breakthrough in AI. Then this would allow AI to design better software and hardware, which would make better AI, which would design increasingly better AI. This positive feedback loop could accelerate very quickly, producing smarter and smarter AI in a short time, much like an atomic chain reaction.

Already, we're at the point where AI can beat the very best human champions in the world in chess and go (an ancient Japanese game of strategy). The designers of these chess and go programs admit that they have very little understanding *how* the AI figures out to play so well. The AI computers are programmed to learn from games, over and over again, until they build their rules and methods for play. The learning can go from a basic 5-year old's understanding of chess to grand master in a matter of hours.

Hypersonic vehicles are similar to ballistic missiles, except they have more of a wing design that allows them to maneuver. Our current ballistic missiles, (both nuclear and high explosive) take a more or less predictable approach that looks a lot like a baseball thrown from center field to home plate. It follows a parabolic trajectory up and back down. Ballistic missiles typically have a range of roughly 100-12,000 miles. The longer the range, the higher and faster they go, just like the baseball analogy above. But because hypersonic vehicles are somewhat maneuverable, they are much harder to shoot down than our current ballistic missiles, meaning that whoever can make these work first will have a big advantage.

**Driving out capital:** Have you ever stopped to wonder why we have such a high standard of living in the US? Why does an American make around $60k a year (median, round numbers) while someone in the Philippines makes about $10k? Are we six times smarter than some other races and ethnic groups? Obviously not. Is it because we work harder? While we do work long hours, many countries work long hours and we certainly don't work six times longer than those in the Philippines. Is it because the country was built up by slaves 150 years ago and we just rode on the wave of stolen labor? Many, in fact most, countries have had slavery and in many cases that makes them poorer because the slaves just work barely hard enough to get by, but they aren't making the effort to be inventive and work extra hard.

Maybe it's because the US is blessed with abundant natural resources? While we do have a lot of some resources, there is very little correlation between a country's resources and national wealth. Many African countries have great resources, yet they are pitifully poor. Russia, Venezuela and Argentina (named after the enormous deposits of silver found there) have abundant resources but their economies are slow and the people are much poorer. Japan, Taiwan and South Korea have very little natural resources, yet they're both nearly as prosperous as the US. What sets apart these wealthy countries, and the US in particular, is that we have had free enterprise and protected property rights with an honest justice system for many years.

For years, capital has been invested in the US, both from US businesses rolling profits back into expansion and foreigners bringing their hard earned money here to make a business. Year after year of compound interest has built up the US and made this the great success story of the world. Driving out capital is the biggest and most important reason that the US will become impoverished, be burdened with a slowing economy and eventually lose their military might and influence around the world.

It's been known for over 200 years that capital is productive. This means that if you've saved up money you can invest it in something like a factory or farmland that gives a stream of future income. This stream of future income is greater than your initial investment (if you invested in something worthwhile) and the difference between your investment and the value of the stream represents your profit or the interest return on your investment. Of course, any undertaking has risk, and this must be factored into the "costs" of your business. But having individuals make their own choices about how to invest is a huge incentive for them to be careful and invest wisely. Their investments, such as building a factory, benefits all of society with cheaper goods and more high paying jobs.

The US has served as a magnet for capital for over 100 years, which has contributed greatly to our tremendous growth in standard of livings. Marxists and others arguing for greater government control ignore the value of all of this capital being invested in the US and benefiting us all. Capital invested in a country makes all of the workers more productive. Consider what one person can accomplish tilling the soil. It isn't worth very much without machinery, but when you add in some capital investment—a tractor, barn, silos—suddenly this one person is vastly more productive. The same things happen when capital is used to build factories, shopping malls, apartment buildings as well as when investing in scientific research. Capital leverages labor, allowing all of us to be much more productive.

However the US Federal Reserve (the Fed) has been on a mission to crush interest rates in recent years, under the misguided Keynesian theory that they can "stimulate" the economy. For most of the past 30 years, the interest rate on the long bond (either 30 or 10 year bonds) has been around 6%. But the Fed has pushed it down to 3% then 2% and very recently (April of 2020) to being less than 1%. You might be thinking "Great! This means that we pay very little of our money on interest!"

But there are other, terrible consequences of having super low rates. You need to know that low interest rates tend to filter through the economy: from T-bonds to municipal bonds to corporate bonds, interest bearing checking accounts and even to stocks. Everything starts paying lower and lower rates. One effect of having very low interest rates is that old people, who have saved and invested through their lives, now get lower and lower monthly payments from their investments, so they grow poorer.

The lower rates also have the effect of punishing savers and driving out capital. Anyone with money to invest will look for other places, outside the US, to park their money. The breakdown of the rule of law, discussed earlier, also leads investors to avoid putting their money in the US. For example, if courts can apply huge and unpredictable billion-dollar settlements on corporations, then corporations are hesitant to invest here. Over time we get progressively less investing, which slows our growth. Japan has gone through this process and they have had a miserable economy for the past 10 or so years. Eventually we'll get this low growth too. So our GDP will stall, but our population will continue to increase.

When you divide a frozen GDP by an ever-increasing number of people, you get lower wages and a lower standard of living. So these artificially low interest rates will make all of us poorer. David Stockman, the former director of the Office of Management and Budget under President Reagan, has repeatedly [57] called for an end to the Federal Reserve's policy of creating artificially low rates. Many other high-profile economists have suggested the same.

Imitation is the most sincere form of compliment. In the beginning of the 1990's, China was a very small economy and not even in the world top-10. But Deng Xiaoping saw the efficiency of a market economy and the value of attracting capital to his country, and partially copied the path to success that had been forged (though forgotten) by the US. Instead of following the Russian model of five year plans and strict central planning, Deng reformed the Chinese economy and allowed some market competition.

Fast forward 30 years and now (2020) China has nearly the same GDP as the US and is set to surpass us in just a few years. Note that making China more of a market economy is in direct violation of the Communist Manifesto's dictum of "government shall control all of the means of production". China is no longer a communist state except in name only. It's more of a fascist, authoritarian country which allows some accumulation of capital by those closely connected to the Communist Party.

I'm not arguing that the US should be like China. Far from it. China is a horrible human rights nightmare. It's an Orwellian surveillance state run by a heavy-handed oligarchy of wealthy families, while the 99% have no individual rights and no real hope of moving upwards. Rather than praising China, I'm merely pointing out that allowing competition and private ownership can cause huge growth. If we Americans abandon what made us great, then we'll pay a terrible price.

China has plenty of problems, and in a way the West should be grateful. Their high preference for having male children, to the point of aborting many female babies, has caused their demographics to be damagingly skewed with many more men than women. Meaning that many men will never have wives and will be miserable. China also has a rather inefficient form of crony-capitalism, where certain families are allowed to dominate certain segments of the economy. Regulators selectively enforce pollution controls and other laws, to the detriment of those who would want to compete with the chosen few.

Even with all of these inefficiencies, China's growth in the past 20-30 years has been truly amazing. The inefficiencies in the US system are large too (huge debt, over-regulation, cronyism, monopolies like the GAFs) and the fact that China manages to attract and retain capital almost as well as the US shows how weakly the US is doing compared to years past.

# Chapter 3:
# How It's Likely to Play Out

———

*"Politics is the art of looking for trouble, finding it everywhere, diagnosing it incorrectly then applying the wrong remedies."* - Groucho Marx [30]

Usually, when the economy and living conditions go downhill, people do all kinds of things that make the situation worse. This string of ill-advised government actions has the cumulative effect of making things fall down the mountain at increasing speed. Two good books that describe the psychodynamics of how things go from bad to worse are *Atlas Shrugged* by Ayn Rand and *The Mandibles* by Lionel Shiver.

The former book is rather dated (written in the 1950's) and deals with an industrial society where railroads and steel manufacture are at the forefront. Still, the principles are very good and the human psychological tendencies are the same now as they were 70 years ago. The latter book is much more contemporary, but shows the same general things unfold. A bad situation leads people to make bad choices, and the country spirals ever deeper into the miserable abyss. Both of those books are enjoyable and insightful. They're worth a read so you'll be aware of the many seemingly plausible solutions that will be proposed and likely enacted into laws, along with how they'll have the unintended consequences of making things worse.

Many of the "solutions" that our politicians will try have already been tried before. And, just like all of the other times, these solutions will fail. The reason that the same things are tried again is a combination of ignorance, naiveté, and cynicism. The public is mostly ignorant because so few schools teach history, and the ones who do mostly bend toward teaching the politically desirable histories (or propaganda) and ignoring everything else. The public is naïve because they believe that some simple fix, such as price controls, will cure the problem of rising prices.

Politicians are often well-educated enough to know that the superficial and seemingly magical "fixes" have been tried before and failed, or at the very least they have knowledgeable staff who will tell them why it won't work. But they don't care. They're cynical enough to feed the lies to the populace in order to get more political power. "Tell the people what they want to hear" was an oft-used approach with cynical orators like Lenin, and it remains popular with US politicians of both the left and right today. Some things never change.

As the economy deteriorates and misery increases look for the government to start downplaying the old metrics like cost of living and unemployment. They will likely create a new metric, perhaps something called the Quality of Life Index which includes such vague and unmeasurable quantities as diversity, tolerance, sustainability, greenness and peace of mind. Naturally, the government will need to consult experts in these fields. The experts will tell us, month after month, how the Quality of Life Index is getting so much better all the time. We should be grateful. If your own quality of life isn't improving, then you must be doing something wrong, or you're some kind of racist or reactionary.

The US will likely become a single-party country in just a few years. I'm writing this in early 2020, during the presidential primary season. The Democratic Party is becoming the "free stuff for everyone party". All of the challengers are eager to promise more free stuff than the others: free college, free food stamps, free healthcare, and free childcare for life. Go ahead and have all the babies you want; the government will happily raise them for you, free of charge.

Have we seen this movie before? Oh yeah, I remember, it was Venezuela in the early 2000's. The country's big export, oil, was doing well and the dictator Hugo Chavez came to power and promised all kinds of free stuff for people. But like socialism/communism has done everywhere, it wrecked their economy. Now Venezuela is incredibly poor and the people are literally starving. But Chavez's chosen successor (not put in office in a fair election), Maduro, is still enjoying power. The misery continues with no end in sight.

The left-wing politicians in the US, and their academic enablers, will keep telling us that "it will be different this time". But it's not different in Russia, Cuba, China (until recently when they abandoned communism, as remarked above), Bolivia, Venezuela and Argentina. In every single case, the country trying it has descended into greater poverty.

If you want to know generally how things will play out in the US, just look toward Venezuela for our future. Oscar Wilde put it well when he said, "*They've promised that dreams would come true, but forgot to mention that nightmares are dreams too.*" As the economy goes down, then things happen at ever-increasing rates.

The US dollar is removed as the world's reserve currency, and inflation comes roaring back. So all cash is removed from society and money becomes electronic, with the bank taking a certain percentage every month in the form of negative interest rates (NIRP). Capital flees the country as many new laws are implemented to crush business (in the guise of helping). Jobs also leave and new jobs are not created because there is no capital being invested. The government sets up many new job-creation organizations. But of course these programs are administered by their friends and are used as political tools to help pay back their supporters, and therefore the jobs created are low paid and not at all efficient in producing anything of value.

Shortages of food and other essentials become common because it isn't worthwhile for farmers and others to produce/sell food. Riots become common, so the government beefs up their security forces everywhere. The government uses most of the available food to make sure that the large police and military forces are well-fed, while most other people go hungry. The propaganda machine works overtime to tell each group that it's the fault of someone else, such as claiming that farmers are illegally withholding food or that hoarders are responsible for the shortages.

Websites will spring up and inform people of the tyranny and government corruption, so the government will pass laws restricting freedom of the press, with severe penalties for spreading "rumors, fake news and disinformation". I use those words with irony because the government will define them to mean "anything that is not in agreement with the official state media". CNN, MSNBC, NPR and the New York Times won't be affected since they already slavishly tow the party line.

As each new miserable development occurs, government will take new powers and enact new policies that make it worse. Individual rights and state's rights as outlined in the Constitution will increasingly diverge from the actual rights in practice. Earlier we talked about the difference between de jure (written) laws and de facto (real) laws. This will become more obvious even to those who have accepted the public school propaganda.

Socialism requires stealing from some people (nearly always the middle class) in order to buy votes from other people (mostly the poor). Votes aren't cheap though. For example, in the 2016 US Presidential election, Hillary Clinton spent about $770 million [66], while Donald Trump spent about $440 million. Clinton got about 66 million votes, for a cost of about $12 per vote, and Trump got 63 million votes, for a cost of $7 per vote. But the cost of the election is still very small compared to the redistribution of wealth schemes that either side will inflict on the already sinking US economy.

H.L. Mencken described it well when he said "*The government consists of a gang of men exactly like you and me. They have, taking one with another, no special talent for the business of government; they have only a talent for getting and holding office. Their principal device to that end is to search out groups who pant and pine for something they can't get and to promise to give it to them. Nine times out of ten that promise is worth nothing. The tenth time is made good by looting A to satisfy B. In other words, government is a broker in pillage, and every election is sort of an advance auction sale of stolen goods.*"

Note that the election costs described earlier don't account for the "hidden contributions". For example Google, Facebook, CNN, NPR and MSNBC promoted stories that made Democrats look good and Republicans look worse. Clinton's scandals, like having an illegal email server and letting hundreds of secret documents fall into foreign hands, were usually sugar-coated or not mentioned at all. Trump's scandals, for example talking dirty about women or sleeping with Stormy Daniels, were at the very top of the news cycle every day for months.

The Democrats are certain to take over in the US, leaving the Republicans with very few seats in the US House and Senate, and with no real power. Even state legislatures in traditionally "red" states like Texas will be dominated by Democrats.

The reason for this revolution will be due to 2 demographic waves. First, old people (conservatives) are dying and young people (hyper liberal) are coming of voting age. Second, due to Democrats in California letting in as many illegal aliens as possible from Mexico, and giving them voting rights, there are vastly more poor people soon to be on the voting rolls. Most of these poor people pay no taxes and don't read history or current events, so are unaware how this movie ends. (It gets ugly.) So they will vote for the most socialist and economically destructive candidates that the Democratic Party has to offer. The rest will play out much like Venezuela.

Nearly every other major country requires government issued ID in order to vote. Texas and other states have tried to have voter ID laws but the Democrats have fought bitterly against any form of ID being used, calling the process "racist" (as they call everything they disagree with). Have you ever wondered why the Democrats fight so hard against ID laws for the US? The simple answer is that illegal aliens vote overwhelmingly Democrat. And no one can challenge them or even find them because it's easy to register to vote with a fictitious address, or even better register multiple times with many addresses.

The trend toward voting by mail also helps the fraud. One person can register at their own home, and at various family members and friend's homes in order to vote many times. This is an open secret, but the Democrats find it an effective path to power. It's no longer really a democracy if your vote can be diluted many times.

Like most of the corrupt third-world countries, the US will become a single-party state. Once the Democrats are in power, they will use their supermajority in Congress as well as their grasp on the presidency in order to further consolidate power. The first effort will be to water down the remaining Senate power of what they like to call the "flyover states" (meaning the states between the coasts. The coasts are liberal strongholds like CA, NY and MA, and the middle states are filled with "deplorables" as Hillary labeled them.)

In order to dilute the small remaining power of the Republicans, Democrats will quickly introduce many new states into the Union: American Samoa, Puerto Rico and Guam for starters. Possibly also DC, Wake Island, the Marshall Islands, the Northern Mariana Islands and the US Virgin Islands. So we could see as many as 8 new states that are admitted in order to severely water down the last of the Republican flyover states in the US Senate.

Part of the problem in admitting all of these new states, and one that will be completely ignored during any debate on the subject, is that they are all on the fringes of the empire and difficult to defend. So the US will spend more and more money each year trying to shore them up to keep them from the up-and-coming Chinese. The Chinese economy continues to grow at a much faster pace than the US (about 6% per year compared to 2% here at home). It's an ancient maxim that from economic power comes military power.

As the Chinese economy eclipses the US, due to our own mismanagement, the Chinese will become evermore aggressive at subtly threatening these far-flung outposts. They'll sail their battleships close to the island and fly reconnaissance flights close by, forcing US fighters to scramble and intercept them. The Chinese can, with a small investment, require the US to spend huge sums to keep up with defending each tiny new state, bleeding even more treasure from the already collapsing US economy. Rome had this same problem with their far-flung empire. It is time to recognize that the US empire is in retreat. We can retreat gracefully and decide just which things are worth defending, or we can retreat in complete disarray and lose everything. That is the choice that we will soon need to make.

Can you imagine the humiliation if the US went from 58 states to 57 because the US had to abandon, for example, Guam after it was hit by Chinese (or their vassal state, North Korean) missiles? There has never before been a time when we had to "erase" a star from the flag, but it could happen in the not too distant future.

The second phase of the Democratic takeover will include packing the US Supreme Court with between 3 and 7 new members that are all chosen to be as far left as possible. The US Constitution doesn't say that the Supreme Court shall be exactly 9 justices, though this has been the custom for over 150 years, since 1869. President Roosevelt tried this technique to pack the court with his supporters in 1934, but the Senate wisely smacked him down. This time however, the Senate will be solidly Democratic and will favor doing what they can to further reduce Republican power by whatever means possible, ethical or not, legal or not.

The third phase and most hardcore part of the Democratic takeover will be to hold a Constitutional convention in order to throw out all of the "outdated" amendments and parts of the Constitution that they've disliked for a long time. The second amendment (gun rights) will obviously be completely discarded with very little debate. The first amendment (freedom of speech) will be gutted in order to outlaw any sort of "hate speech" or "fake news". Of course, in order to determine exactly what news is fake, we'll need to have "experts" appointed to a kind of Ministry of Truth (taken from George Orwell's 1984). The name Ministry of Truth won't be used, of course, but it will have the same effect and the same powers to get rid of any unwanted criticism or discussion.

This might seem extreme, with the Democrats moving to restrict free speech, but remember that we've enjoyed a divided government for a long time so one side wasn't allowed to totally dominate. Without the Republican "obstructionists" (as Obama called them) the true social engineers of the Democrats will come shining through. Also, it's important to remember that the ANTIFA movement has repeatedly tried to crush free speech, and that group is very closely aligned with Democratic party interests.

ANTIFA is effectively the militant wing of the Democratic Party, and has a large base of support among the farther left portion of the party.

Joe Biden has repeatedly praised them [24], even though this group has attacked anyone who disagrees with the hardcore Democrats, including journalists and peaceful free-speech groups. It's not completely unimaginable that ANTIFA would receive more money from the US government (or the billionaires behind those in power) and be used as a plausibly deniable tool to get rid of dissent.

The US government could, for example, secretly support ANTIFA, and simultaneously create a few well-publicized show-trials against ANTIFA members so they can claim to be against anyone who would use violence to stop free speech. These show trials would merely be a way to weed out the parts of ANTIFA that refused to go along and in order to consolidate power. If you want to see how the Democratic Party will treat ANTIFA after they're no longer useful, read up on how Hitler treated the "Brownshirts" (aka Sturmabteilung) and killed his former friend Ernst Rohm when the latter became too powerful.

Another part of the Constitution that Democrats hate is the Electoral College. Without the Electoral College, Hillary would have won the 2016 election and Democrats have not forgotten this. Here's a tiny bit of history on the Electoral College. When the original union was being formed, there were some very large states like New York and Massachusetts, and some very small ones like Rhode Island and Delaware. The large states wanted any representation to be strictly proportional to population. But the small states feared, quite legitimately, that they would become insignificant and that their interests or rights would be ignored if only the large states mattered. The small states threatened to refuse to join the new union, rather favoring to remain independent countries, if it was going to be a strictly mob rule sort of arrangement.

The compromise was to have two houses of Congress: The House of Representatives (being strictly proportional to population) and the

Senate (where each state has equal say with 2 representatives per state). The Electoral College then was to give voting power as the sum of these: the number of House seats plus 2 for each state. The Electoral College then required that any candidate for president must simultaneously try to appeal to a large percent of the population, but also try to appeal to the small and ignored states. But the Democrats prefer a strictly mob rule, whereby the election is decided by the large coastal cities, and so the Electoral College will be unceremoniously killed with very little debate.

You can expect a lot of tax increases once the Democrats are the single party in power. But the tax increases will nearly all be directed at the middle class. The poor have no money to steal. The rich have lawyers, trust funds, foundations, offshore accounts and other ways of defending themselves, making them a hard target, so they'll get only small and token tax increases. Sure, politicians will spin the latest tax bill as being out to "soak the rich", but when you look at it closely you'll find that they define "rich" as a family making over 50k per year. It's important to remember that the Democrats are a coalition of the very rich and very poor, so those groups will generally be spared while the middle class will pay most of these taxes.

You should also expect some tricky and hidden new taxes. For example, on the state and local levels, politicians intentionally neglect roads so that people are screaming for something to be done. Even though population goes up every year, and in some cities like Austin, TX, it's doubled in the past 20 years, the small roads are kept at two lanes even though many new subdivisions are all feeding traffic into those same old roads. The politicians are happy with all of the new tax revenue that comes with the new influx of jobs and population, but they neglect the roads anyway. Then, after people have complained for long enough, they introduce new bond issues to pay for roads, leaving the taxpayers to pay for a bond with higher property or sales taxes for 20-30 years.

But then soon after completing it, politicians sell off that same road to private developers who turn it into a toll road. Then the taxpayers end up paying for the same road twice! Did you notice the bait and switch here? The politicians promised that the bond issue would go toward roads, but after the road was built, the politicians sold the road and then used the money for some other political mischief like shoes for the dead [65] (since their friends own a shoe factory). The citizens would never have approved of an extra tax (bond issue) to pay for the shoes, but the politicians got them anyway by promising to use the money to pay for the long-neglected roads.

The local governments also neglect building schools for the large number of new residents. They pack progressively more students in each classroom, stretching teachers ever thinner. The politicians enjoy all of the extra tax revenue from the many new residents, but they ignore this extra revenue and point out only the extra costs of the schools. Then they argue for a great new bond issue or property tax increase to pay for the schools. The politicians keep increasing taxes in various tricky ways.

Other hidden taxes include the AMT (alternative minimum tax). When this tax was created in 1968, it was promised that it would affect only a tiny number of people in the highest tax brackets. But since the level at which the tax kicks in was not indexed for inflation, each year it would affect more and more people, eventually soaking the middle class (of course). Part of Trump tax reform of 2017 moved this tax back up to only affect people making over 200k, but those in power will soon pass laws to remove the tax cuts, and reset the AMT so that it affects the middle class once again.

Another hidden tax can be found in Obamacare. In fact, the Supreme Court was forced to admit that Obamacare was indeed a big new tax when they upheld it in 2012. By forcing employers to pay for this expensive new program, the employers were then forced to pass on the tax to their customers or by cutting worker's wages. But the workers didn't see how that happened. They see the goodies in subsidized healthcare, but then don't understand why prices went up, wages went down and jobs were scaled back or never created. The middle-class workers also paid for Obamacare by way of higher monthly premiums, greatly increased deductibles and higher coinsurance costs (i.e. the percentage that you pay for hospital and surgery fees).

As mentioned earlier, this coming Blue Wave demographic shift will allow Democrats to have super majorities in all three branches of the federal government: president, Congress and Supreme Court. Some people will criticize this characterization by noting that Supreme Court judges are not explicitly partisan. But when you look at the important Supreme Court decisions, they nearly always split along party lines with those who were appointed by Republicans voting the Republican side and those who were appointed by Democrats nearly always uphold the Democrat side. So much for the charade that they're impartial and non-partisan referees who are only intent on upholding the Constitution.

Since the Democrats will appoint 3-5 new SCOTUS (Supreme Court of the United States) judges in order to pack the court, this will allow them to control how the laws are upheld and which old laws are thrown out without having to do any kind of embarrassing legislation or actually voting on the new laws. The super majority in government will also extend to most state governments and even local governments, as people mindlessly vote a straight Democratic ballot from top to bottom.

But things will not be all hugs and rainbows for the new Democratic masters of the country because no sooner will they have complete control and start on their path to domination than they will begin the internal battles. You can already see this happening in the state of California. Because they have proportional primaries where both parties can vote, then the top two in the primary face off for the general election, the only people you see on the ballot are Democrats. Then you see Democrats viciously attacking Democrats. The candidates take turns promising more and more free stuff for everyone to the point of absurdity. You might think of them as the Silly Party and the Very Silly Party [76], if you're a Monty Python fan.

H.L. Mencken put it well when he said *"The urge to save humanity is almost always a false front for the urge to rule."* The Democratic Party itself is an extremely heterogeneous mixture of different groups and special interests, often with conflicting goals. Sometimes it's surprising that they've managed to stay together all this time, which is why they need the Republican Party to act as a foil for as long as possible, or as a threat to keep their own many small groups in line. But the strain will become too great to bear when they finally get their heart's desire and secure supermajorities everywhere and make Republicans powerless. There are too many small tyrants in the party who have this urge to rule, and so there will be a lot of infighting in the Democratic Party.

When the Democrats are on the verge of splitting into two parties, or soon thereafter, you should watch for leaders of one or both parties to suddenly vanish or have some terrible accident or "suicide". I use the word suicide loosely, rather like Jeffrey Epstein committed suicide. That was very convenient for some people that he killed himself so quickly before he could reveal too much, don't you agree?

There are various websites where people have documented the large number of Clinton associates and investigators who have committed suicide or died mysteriously [62]. Soon after Lenin died in 1924, there was a falling out and power struggle between Stalin and Trotsky. Trotsky lost and was exiled or fled, eventually making it to Mexico. This wasn't far enough away for Stalin, who had his henchman find him and execute him. This is a bit of a simplification and leaves out many details, such as the many countries that Trotsky went to along the way, but you get the idea.

It's a common practice in power struggles to kill off one's rivals, so it's an easy guess that others will meet a similar fate. There is just too much power at stake and too many would-be Messiah's for this not to happen. The people who say "it can't happen here" are merely naïve or brainwashed to believe that the modern justice system has anything to do with justice.

In order to pay for at least part of the many promised new benefits and freebies, the government will print a lot of extra money. Okay, these days it's anachronistic to say "print", since the money is created electronically rather than using an actual printing press, but it has the same effect: inflation and price increases. If you look at Venezuela in the 2000's or Germany in the early 1920's, you will see that inflation effects different groups differently.

Food prices generally increase faster than other prices, since everyone has to buy food to survive. Farmers generally suffered less during the historic periods of inflation because they could grow their own food. There's no point in selling your food to market for money that is worth close to nothing, but at least you can eat what you grow and barter other parts of it to your neighbors for beef, pork, eggs and whatever they have.

When inflation was high in Germany in the early part of the 20$^{th}$ century, or Venezuela in the early 21$^{st}$ century, different groups turned against each other. Naturally, government likes this sort of chaos because it's easy to get people emotional and hating (without thinking about) other groups. For example, farmers ate most of the food they produced because they couldn't buy very much with the money that the food would bring at market. And so the government blamed (and in Venezuela, continue to blame) farmers for "withholding" food from the market. City people blamed country people. Professionals blamed union workers and, in Germany of the 1920's, everyone blamed the Jews.

All of this plays into the hands of politicians who want to stir up a lot of misery and anger in order to implement extreme policies. Of course, this time it won't be blamed on the Jews. That trick has been tried and is too transparent to use again, at least not so soon. Instead, they'll blame straight white males for unfairly profiting from slavery and keeping down women as well as minorities.

During periods of high inflation, most money and paper assets will be wiped out. This is a form of theft from the government, since money is basically a contract between you and the government whereby they agree to let you store some of your labor for future use. But by inflating the currency, government is sneakily, quietly, stealing it from you. People who owned their own home did better than most in times when inflation was high. Holding a lot of debt to buy a house might seem like a good idea, since that debt will be made smaller by inflation.

However, there have been times when governments have created a new currency, such as the German Roggenmark (tied to the price of rye, a popular crop in the area) and Rentenmark (tied to the price of rent or mortgages). The unfortunate thing was that when the new mark was introduced, people who had mortgages in the old marks saw their mortgages reformed in the new mark, which effectively made their mortgages reset to the newer and higher priced marks.

In this case, many people didn't benefit from the inflation reducing their debt. Only the government and their close friends could see their own debt reduced by inflation. So there are precedents where mortgages were "reset" in order to help the banks, and it could happen here making it difficult to pay your mortgage because most of your income would go toward food. It benefits you to have low debt levels.

During the German inflation of the 1920's, the value of the stock market approximately kept pace with inflation, at least during the early stages. But eventually the stock market too lost most of its value because businesses couldn't operate under the terrible economic condition. The stock market didn't fall in value in a smooth and predictable straight line, but there were times when the stock market (and the value of the German mark) had rallies as much as 30-40%. There were even uneducated people who thought the mark would "come back from these troubles". When it happens here, don't be fooled: paper money eventually always goes to zero. Be happy to sell during the rallies.

In the example of German hyperinflation, public workers and unionized laborers suffered somewhat but generally fared better than most since their wages at least partly kept up with inflation. This still isn't good, as even their standard of living fell behind, just to a lesser degree. Professionals like doctors and engineers did worse, since they didn't get the monthly or weekly wage increases to partly offset inflation. Pensioners and others on fixed incomes did the worst of all. Their savings were wiped out and their pension or social security (or equivalent government payments) were generally much lower than the official government numbers on the cost of living. Learn from history and plan accordingly.

In the US in the 1970's we had ruinous inflation (around 10% per year). This was partly caused by the administration of President Johnson choosing the path of "guns and butter". This meant that they would spend a lot of money on the military (the guns portion) to support the Vietnam War and they would also greatly increase social welfare spending (the butter portion), avoiding the hard choices of which things to fund most. The huge spending increases would all be facilitated with a large increase in government borrowing together with printing money.

Johnson also debased the currency by removing all silver from US coins in 1964. Interestingly, the government tried to perpetuate a scam where they made the new dimes, quarters and half-dollars look like the old silver coins by making a sandwich with nickel on the outside and copper inside. This became known, somewhat derisively, as a "Johnson sandwich".

President Nixon inherited this slow economy and high inflation (stagflation, as it was called) from the poor fiscal policies of the Johnson administration. As is typical of big-government supporters, Nixon implemented a policy that would only make things worse: wage and price controls [27]. These have been tried throughout history, going back at least to the Roman Empire [28] and probably beyond, and they've always failed. It's well-known that wage and price controls just cause shortages when they're used to hold down prices. At the artificially created price (as opposed to a fair market price determined by both buyers and sellers), there are too few sellers who are willing to sell at that price and there are far too many buyers. Price controls are popular with buyers until they realize that they have to stand in line for hours to get one loaf of bread at the bargain price, or even that they can't find any at all for the official price (i.e. shortages).

During the Ford presidency years, around 1974, the government still had the same problems of stagflation. Ford continued to use the same poor fiscal policies and overspent even more. Again the Federal Reserve was called upon to monetize the debt (or create money out of nothing to pay for it). And again inflation increased even while the economy was slow and millions were out of work.

This time the government went on a huge advertising campaign to try to convince people that inflation was just the result of greedy people and businesses increasing prices. Part of this silly process was the creation of the WIN or Whip Inflation Now buttons. This whole process was just another one of government misdirection, avoiding responsibility for the destructive fiscal policies that they themselves created, supported and worked to expand.

Inflation is one form of attack (or subtle theft) on savings. ZIRP (zero interest rate policy) is another such attack. Currently ( early 2020) in the US, we have close to zero interest rates as the Federal Reserve pushes rates lower and lower in an effort to revive an economy that is being dragged down by the weight of debt, taxes and over-regulation. Old people who have saved their whole lives find that the return they get on conservative investments, such as bonds or bank accounts, pays very little of their monthly bills. Sure, there's also Social Security, but that's already small and will soon be cut or fail to keep up with actual cost of living increases.

Banks generally fare direly under ZIRP. Few people will want to put their money in the bank and get no return. Instead, people just buy stocks or real estate such as a home. Banks can borrow short term money from the Federal Reserve discount window for very low rates, then loan it out at 4% for mortgages, which seems attractive until you realize that the 4% might not keep pace with inflation. In that situation, banks are losing money every month. If the short term rates ever go up, banks are forced to roll over their debt by borrowing again and could end up borrowing at higher rates than they have those 30-year mortgage money loaned out.

You might not personally care very much about your banks financial health, but you should. Many people aren't aware of this, but when you loan money to a bank (by opening a checking or savings account), there's no iron-clad guarantee that you'll get your money back. You're just one more creditor, like the electric company, who has to stand in line in hopes of getting part of your money back when a bank fails.

In order to keep banks solvent, inventive governments around the world have sometimes relied on what are called "bail-ins". This is where the bank, under protection by the government, takes a certain amount from each account. This happened a few years ago in Cyprus [33], where the banks were in trouble due to many risky loans made to Greece and others. The banks ended up taking about 10% of depositor money.

You might think that the FDIC (Federal Deposit Insurance Corporation) in the US would protect you from this. People in Cyprus thought that too, unworried because they expected that they were covered by their equivalent governmental program. But this is a special government action, sometimes labeled as a tax, and it's immune to FDIC reimbursement. A bail-in is a sneaky way for government to get around having to reimburse people via the FDIC or other national insurance programs.

Another even more fiendish way to steal money from savers is NIRP (negative interest rate policy). The idea here is that any money you have in a bank or savings and loan pays not zero but a negative rate of return. So you have $5,000 in your account at the start of the month but you lose 1%, so at the end of the month you now have $4,950. You might think to yourself "Ha! I'd never fall for that. I'd just take out all my money in cash, put it in a lock box and be good. At least I wouldn't lose money then." This is where making all money electronic comes in. If governments can get rid of all cash, then your paycheck will be electronically deposited in your bank account and you'll use a debit card to buy everything. It's simple and convenient, and many of us do this all the time already.

To many people it might seem like a small step to simply make all money electronic and get rid of cash and coins entirely. The trouble is that when *all* money is electronic, then it becomes much easier to implement this marvel of Modern Monetary Theory: NIRP. Cash will no longer exist, so you won't be able to protect yourself from this type of theft. There is a lot of money sitting in millions of bank accounts around the US, and as the US government grows more desperate to fund everything, it is almost irresistible to just help themselves to a little bit of the money each month.

Your money is much easier to steal, by banks and the government, when it's held by the bank in electronic form. And this is precisely why big-government types and supporters of MMT are all in favor of the combination of NIRP and electronic money. The central theme of socialism is that it relies on using OPM (other people's money) to buy votes. As Margaret Thatcher famously said "*The problem with socialism is that you eventually run out of other people's money* [34]."

Naturally, the redistribution of wealth crowd won't admit that this is how the game is played, so you can look forward to them creating lots of big scandals involving cash, such as drugs or prostitution or bribery. They'll blame it on cash and their media lackeys will parrot this message over and over in their campaign to force money to be electronic.

When the economy starts to go down, our masters in Washington will notice the "capital flight", meaning that people are taking money out of the country to invest it abroad. They'll talk to their political friends and ask what can be done. The obvious solution: make it illegal or very expensive (by way of taxes) to take money out. But this addresses only the symptom and makes the underlying problem much worse, just like enacting price controls. Of course, if they had asked economists if capital controls were a good idea, nearly all of them (except the Modern Monetary Theory snake oil salesmen) would tell them that capital controls have been tried by many countries in many different time periods, and are always highly destructive to the economy.

Think about it: If you were a billionaire in another country, would you want to invest in the US knowing that you could never bring your money back out? Of course you wouldn't. But our political leaders only think in terms of the next sound bite, hoping they'll look good on the evening news or their next careless tweet on Twitter. This would be a desperate attempt to save the economy that they destroyed by their many other ruinous policies, and things will get much worse when capital controls become law.

Perhaps surprisingly, the Democrats will need to keep the Republicans around. They'll need someone to scare the populace, a kind of scarecrow. The implication will be something like, "You need to keep backing Democrats, or those evil Republicans will bring back racism and income inequality". Never mind that income inequality grew worse even under the watch of Saint Obama. The Democrats will need this Republican bogeyman in order to keep their own party together for a little longer.

As the economy starts to go down and people realize that it's a one-party state, and that single party isn't making the economy any better, then the Democrats will start blaming each other. For a while they'll blame Trump and global warming and their other love-to-hate poltergeists, but that will start to wear thin when the single-party state has been in effect for 4-5 years.

Currently, the billionaires largely support Democrats because that party gives them the most favors for their money. But as the Democratic Party threatens to split into two parties, then many billionaires will switch to quietly giving money to Republicans. The idea here is that they need to at least make the Republicans a recognized presence in the elections so it's less obviously a single-party state. The Democrats will certainly keep all of the real power, but they'll work to elect a Republican here and there just for show. They'll need a scapegoat and scarecrow as I mentioned earlier. This ruse will only work for a limited time, and eventually the Democrats will break up, perhaps calling themselves the Democratic Socialists or Progressives versus the Moderate Democrats or Obamacrats (in an effort to try to conjure up images of the good old days before the economy soured).

Social security has been on a trajectory of doom for at least 30 years. It's been well-known that they wouldn't be able to meet their obligations in the future since at least the 1980's. It was a sweet deal when it started in 1935, with old people that year getting money even though they never paid anything in. Even people in the 1940's paid very little in and got a lot back. The system was always a redistribution of wealth scheme where current workers all pay a tax (currently around 15% of income) and this money then gets sent to the retirees. It should be noted that the 15% tax is split between employee and employer, but in the end it reduces employee wages and increases costs to the consumer.

Do a thought experiment where the government enacts a new 10% tax on all employers based on the money they pay their workers. This money has to come from somewhere, so the employer responds by paying workers less and charging the consumers more. It can't be any other way.

The SS system worked okay-ish in the 1950's because there were many workers and few retirees. But as there gradually became more old people and the number of workers grew much slower, it became apparent that the system was in trouble. Originally, there were about 41 workers paying in for each one that took money out, giving an apparent surplus. However, this wasn't a real surplus because all of those people who paid in expected to get money back when they got old.

Politicians couldn't help but salivate over all of this "extra" money in the Social Security Trust Fund, so they devised lots of new benefits: child benefits, widows, disabled. It quickly became apparent that there would be a huge problem paying all of these benefits in the future. But politicians only think about the next election. What was going to happen in 10-20 years was no concern, so they quickly passed lots of generous new benefits.

Here we are in 2020 with only 2.9 workers paying in for each person receiving benefits. And it's expected to get worse, eventually reaching 1:1. There are essentially only two possible solutions to this:

1. Decrease benefits.
2. Increase taxes.

For 30 years, no one wanted to talk about Social Security. In political circles they joked about it being the "third rail" (a reference to the high voltage rail for subways and electric trains) meaning that it was instant political death for anyone to touch it. So all politicians ignored it, pushing the problem into the future where someone else would have to deal with it. Very soon, the SS problem won't be able to be ignored because it will consume more and more of the Federal Budget in order to cover the shortfall.

For the first few years it will just be added onto the ever-growing Federal Debt. As the problem grows with each passing year then politicians will be forced to do something, and will probably choose a combination of increased taxes and reduced benefits.

One way to reduce benefits is to keep increasing the retirement age, currently at 67 years old for someone born in 1960 (a few months less for those older). So the retirement age will keep rising even as you keep chasing it as you get older. The SS system also gives incentives, in the form of 24% bigger checks, if you wait to take benefits until you're 70.

Superficially, this looks like a good deal because you get 24% larger checks every month. There are several reasons why this might end up being a poor deal for most people, and I'll cover this in the next chapter.

A tricky way for the federal government to get their hands on more money to cover the SS shortfall, at least for a few years, is for them to seize private pensions. I'll describe how this trick will work, and why it will impoverish many more people that it ever helps. First, there will be a few companies that declare bankruptcy and can't pay their pensions. Many companies have invested money for their workers' retirements but these pensions are not fully funded, meaning that the company will either have to put up a lot of extra money each year to cover the pension shortfall, or will have to declare bankruptcy.

A few companies will indeed declare bankruptcy and some people might get only 50% of their promised pension. This will be on CNN and other billionaire-sponsored news media over and over again, every 15 minutes, showing close up pictures of pensioners eating canned dog food and begging on the streets. You know they can find at least one person like this, and that's all it takes for a good visual or an interview on NPR. Never mind that it's not typical, or even very common.

After the public is disgusted and saddened by these images of piteous old people for a while, there will be a call for the government to "do something". Happily, our official state planners will step in with a self-serving plan. They'll pass laws to take over ALL pensions, saying that workers shouldn't be put at such risk by having their futures in the hands of unscrupulous employers.

Note that the government gets all of the good pensions that are fully (or even 110%) funded as well as the ones only funded 50%. They get a big pot of money NOW in order to do political mischief and then all of the obligations (paying out pensions) occur 10-30 years from now. This apparent windfall in the short term is used to keep SS going for another 5 years or so, but when things come due the payouts will be much more than they took in. The big windfall of stealing pensions will also be used to help pay for the Free Stuff For Everyone agenda.

An overlooked problem with the government taking pensions is that they can now fashion new rules, purportedly in the interest of fairness, in order to help some groups and hurt others. They can take money from the well-run companies' pension funds, and use that to pay for the poorly run pension funds, as well as to help out SS. The feds can also increase retirement ages for these pensions, which is a form of reducing benefits. After all, so they'll say, it's unfair if a person working at one company can retire at 55 while someone working at another company has to wait until age 65 to retire.

As the money quickly runs out to pay for the private pensions and SS, then the feds can introduce more rules that prohibit "double-dipping", as it will be called. You can get a pension *or* SS, but not both. It doesn't matter if you worked for 35 years and made less money in order to get a good pension, you'll get exactly the same as someone who got all of their pay immediately and had no pension at all. Politicians have endless redistribution of wealth schemes in order to buy votes.

In addition to the federal debt and the federal budget deficit, there's another little-known problem of individual states having a great deal of difficulty paying their bills. Oftentimes, this is the result of politicians offering increasingly generous benefits for public employees. After all, these employees are a big voting bloc, so giving them freebies (paid for by the other taxpayers) is another good way to buy votes by using OPM. The promised benefits are delivered right now while the cost is all in the future, making it even easier for politicians to use this to win elections now and let someone else deal with the problem of how to pay for it later.

Eventually, some states will be close to bankruptcy and come to the federal government, with their hat in their hands, asking for a handout or bond guarantees or other help. Note that bond guarantees are just one more way of pushing the cost (plus interest) into the future. If you look at a map [36] of the most fiscally responsible states along with the least responsible, you notice that the ones most likely to need the handouts (CA, IL, NY) are Blue (i.e. controlled by Democrats) while the Red states are, in general, the ones who are living within their means. But when the federal government gives the handouts to the Blue states, it will effectively be yet another transfer of wealth because the Reds will be the ones to pay while receiving little or no help.

The way this debt catastrophe is likely to play out is that CA will feign surprise that they somehow don't have enough tax revenue and need a "temporary" loan or bond guarantee in order to get the debt rescheduled, and to have time to get their house in order. As mentioned earlier, a bond guarantee is just another way to push the problem into the future. By the time when states are on the verge of bankruptcy and come begging, the federal government will be a Democratic one-party state and won't have the political will to say "no" to the largest block of votes in the country. And so the CA debt will be guaranteed.

In short order NY, IL, NJ and MA will also come around asking for their handout. After all, what incentive is there for politicians in these states to make the hard choices between cutting spending or increasing taxes? Eventually it will be advantageous for most of the other states to not bother with the hard work of balancing their own state budgets. There are votes to be gained by giving out more money, as well as votes to be lost by imposing new taxes, and politicians are very aware of this. None of these states will ever bother to get their house in order, though they'll make a big show of trying just as Greece did when they had their own problems.

A whole book could be written just on the topic of how the politics plays out for debt rescheduling, but for more information read about the Greek debt crisis of 2010-2020. No politician wants to be the one to push for "austerity", and so the handout will be taken and then the same states will be back on the brink of bankruptcy in a few more years. Naturally they'll have to act very surprised that they were unable to implement the agreed upon changes, and so they blame it on global warming, Trump or racism. Getting one's house in order requires making hard choices, such as cutting benefits and raising taxes. None of the politicians will go down this path, so in effect all of the state debt will get piled onto the federal debt in short order.

Do you notice how this same trick occurs over and over: politicians deliver wonderful benefits immediately, receiving much credit and getting voted back into office, but the costs are pushed into the future? Politicians aren't very imaginative, so they do the same tricks many times in many different forms, hoping the public can be convinced to "pay no attention to the man behind the curtain". When the cost comes due, with compound interest added, the politicians hold their palms up and say, "We don't know how this happened!". Even though it was their own party who voted for these destructive policies, no one takes responsibility.

When economies are destroyed, such as in the examples of Venezuela and Germany above, the crime rates go way up. There will be many more property crimes in the US, such as theft and burglary. But police will be under a lot of pressure to downplay these and make it hard for people to report them. For example, you often have to report small things online, and it's well-known that no one will ever bother reading about your reported burglary much less actually investigating it or catching the thieves. They make their systems intentionally hard to use and require you to type up a lot of details, which discourages people from even bothering to report. Not reporting is the desired goal of the police departments because it makes the crime statistics better.

I'm not meaning to downplay the emotional damage done by burglaries. I know firsthand that it makes you feel vulnerable and on-edge. Most of us think of our homes as our castles, our safe places where we can go and relax. But when you've been burglarized you no longer feel safe even in your own home and it affects how you feel the rest of your life. Every little noise wakes you up for months thereafter. When you come home from a trip you're not sure if you should go inside, wondering if someone violent is waiting there for you.

With each passing year, the police are increasingly more interested in getting big drug busts that net a lot of money, or catching some would-be terrorist in order to get the glory of being on television. This is part of the problem of making the police become more and more politicized. They chase money and publicity, just like our elected officials. There just isn't any money in protecting people or catching small-time criminals, and this trend will continue to grow worse as the economy falls.

As the country becomes a single-party state (like China, Russia and Iran) and drifts farther toward tyranny, individual rights will be reduced such as the ability to own guns to defend yourself or the right to be served with a search warrant before the government can spy on you. Eventually there will be some people who demonstrate against the regime. Police will brutally put down any sort of grassroots efforts, and eventually these groups of people will also start fighting back against the brutality.

As food becomes scarce, as in Venezuela, the militaristic police will be given most of the available food in order to buy their continued loyalty. The aristocracy in charge will greatly encourage the police to have an "us versus them" mentality. The news media will foster the attitude that all of the protesters are trying to kill police and make the police feel they're in a state of war. It benefits our masters in DC to create an atmosphere of "us against them" between the police and the unwashed crowds. The police can be made to feel that they're under siege and therefore they will become more willing to use violence against the hungry protesters.

You'll see the ANTIFA group grow and they'll be used to violently put down any anti-government protests. The government will have to pretend that this group is operating outside the official control, but in reality they currently are and will continue to be the military wing of the Democratic Party. The government will say things such as not supporting violence against free speech, but then they'll also not prosecute the ANTIFA members who beat and kill the opposition. Police will be instructed to not interfere while ANTIFA is "doing their job". Read about Mussolini's Blackshirts and Hitler's Brownshirts to learn more about how this doublespeak works. Eventually, when the Democrats have crushed all dissent, ANTIFA will be a dangerous threat to power. Eventually, they'll invent some big excuse to jail or kill all of the ANTIFA leadership and install their own leaders who are more passive.

The groups speaking out against the government will be labeled racist or terrorist, since those are the hot-button keywords that tell the average person they can stop thinking and move on. News media will be increasingly pressured to not report anything that shows the protesters in a favorable light, and any who do will run afoul of the new "fake news" laws and have their press passes or broadcasting licenses canceled.

When the leaders or members of any resistance groups speak, their words will be quoted grossly out of context and any videos will make them look as nefarious as possible. For example, the news media will show resistance members fighting back against ANTIFA, but will not show the group marching peacefully and then being attacked by ANTIFA as the police stand by and watch. Deep Fake videos [75] will become more common too and be almost indistinguishable from reality. You'll need to exercise a lot of skepticism and critical thought toward the news media.

If Deep Fake videos didn't exist, the police state would need to create the capability. Over the next few years you'll be bombarded with more and more fake videos, perhaps of Trump eating a live chicken or Biden riding a skateboard like Tony Hawk just to demonstrate how manly he is. Gradually, people will come to question *all* videos. When people get an authentic video of Trump or Biden actually saying something dumb, then their supporters won't accept it and will label it "fake".

This is exactly the situation that's desired by the police state. This way, when the police are caught red-handed beating a handcuffed suspect, the police can just claim that the video is fake. Deny, deny, deny will be the order of the day. And video evidence will no longer convince anyone unless they already believe in whatever is being sold. The existence of Deep Fake videos will cast enough doubt that various wrongdoers can hide behind the possibility, since people will no longer respect any videos.

As Edgar Allen Poe said: "*Believe only half of what you see, and nothing of what you hear.*" Another good quote that applies comes from the 1990's website called Cult of the Dead Cow (and before that from the civil rights movements of the 1970's): "*The revolution will not be televised.*"

# Chapter 4:
# What You Need to Be Doing Now

———

*"Everyone has a plan until they get punched in the mouth."* - Mike Tyson, boxing champion

The first thing you need to be doing now is to develop mental toughness. Yes, life will punch you in the mouth. But you need to be mentally tough and focused like Mike Tyson and keep your wits, keep your intentions, and keep fighting. You need to be resilient and bounce back. You need to introspect and look inside yourself to know what your strengths and weaknesses are. Prepare yourself for what you need to do.

You should also be getting educated on what has happened in the past so you know what tricks governments will try and how to protect yourself and your family for what will come next. This book is a good start on your education, but I've really only touched the highlights of the history of how empires crumble and die. You need to read up on a broad range of subjects and ideas in order to be prepared.

One of the best skills or habits you can cultivate is critical thinking. My late father-in-law used to say, *"Everyone is selling something."* Government, and their hired henchmen such as actors and news readers, will always be spinning the truth. They'll always be trying to convince you that the latest problems and your personal misery are because of someone else or some group. During their speeches to group A they'll blame group B, and when talking to group B they'll blame group A.

During the 1960's people had the slogan "question authority". But curiously, now that the radicals are in power they want you to forget about all of that and just blindly accept whatever the news reader, academic, scientist or self-proclaimed "expert" tells you to believe. And if you don't believe it then you must be a climate change denier, racist, Russian mole, unpatriotic or whatever label works this week to discredit their critics.

Try to practice your critical thinking skills. Always ask yourself, "What are they selling? What are they trying to convince me of?" Then follow the money. Think of who has what to gain by getting you to follow their point of view. If you only watch CNN or MSNBC and listen to NPR on the radio, you'll get a very one-sided view of the world. Get your news from many sources, including foreign websites. Naturally, the large corporate-owned media empires will try to label any alternate sources as "fake news" or fringe or racist.

If they indeed are racist, then you can sort those out very easily. But if they're merely labeled racist and you don't see anything racist, then rest assured that it's a website which presents information that the mainstream wants to keep away from you. Many popular websites aren't very reliable, particularly for any information that touches on the edges of politics, such as economics, current affairs or academia. Wikipedia and Snopes are both very biased when it comes to anything political, and have been repeatedly discredited [84], [85].

In order to be prepared to handle what might come your way, you need to have the right people in your life. Just as importantly, you need to remove the wrong people: those who cause strife and drama, overly negative people, addicts (drugs, alcohol, television, credit cards, etc.) and the energy vampires who just want to drag you down.

It's always good to invest in yourself. You can get education and experience in things that will be useful to yourself and your family after the economy collapses. There are inexpensive college classes you can take at night or online. There are also many YouTube videos on every imaginable subject. You might consider learning more about first aid, gardening and raising chickens. Learn which herbs are medicinal and which herbs you like for flavoring that also grow well in your locale. From my experience, basil and mint both grow very heartily in the Southwest.

**Prepping.** Being a prepper is gaining a reputation in the media as something done by racist groups. If the billionaire-owned media is this much against it, then it's probably a good idea. Note that they call everything they disagree with "racist"; it's just the knee-jerk thing our masters do so that many of the TV-watching sheep will just accept it without having to think about it very long.

There are many things you can buy cheaply now that might be difficult to get or will be expensive later. I suggest having at least a handgun and maybe a rifle for your home defense. And don't forget your ammo. I'd recommend using common sizes like .357 magnum, .38 special, .45ACP and 9mm for your handguns and 0.223 for the rifle. These sizes have good chances of being available for barter later. The 0.22 rifle is very good against small game (rabbits, quail) and the ammo is cheap, but it's poor for self-defense. Still, I keep a 0.22 as a second or third one in my collection, but if you plan to get just one gun then get something bigger.

Some foods you might want to consider buying and holding are: grains like rice or wheat, dried pasta, dried beans, cooking oil, and sugar or honey. Canned meats such as tuna, chicken, Spam, corned beef and mackerel are good sources of protein. Many preppers also keep a stock of multi-vitamins, Tang (for vitamin C and a glucose boost) as well as canned vegetables. All of these things can last a very long time if properly stored.

Other non-food items you can keep a long time and might be valuable after economic decline are spirits (vodka, whiskey, rum), toilet paper and expendable car parts such as oil filters, breaks and belts. There are a number of medical supplies that can be gotten cheaply now at Walmart or even your local dollar store, and could help you immensely later: Pepto Bismal, Advil, Tylenol, Tums, Benadryl. As well as assorted first-aid items such as Band-aids, alcohol pads, Neosporin, and so forth. I'm using brand names here but it's fine to use the generic or store versions of these.

**Minimalism and a more secure financial position.** You should be considering your financial situation and just how well it could stand up to problems that might occur. Try to live a minimalistic life while saving a lot of your paycheck. It's more a matter of your mental attitude than anything. *"True contentment is not in having everything, but being satisfied with everything you have."* – Oscar Wilde.

You might find that minimalistic living is actually easier than having lots of stuff. It's a simpler life with fewer worries. Having fewer belongings means it's easier to find what you need rather than having to go through endless boxes in the attic or garage. And if you're one of the millions of Americans who rents one of the popular storage spaces, consider how much money you could be saving by downsizing.

When I suggest that you save money, this might seem like a contradiction to my earlier warning about the banks doing bail-ins and NIRP (negative interest rate policy). However, you should become creative and not keep most of your savings in the bank, but rather be saving in other ways. You can be a prepper and start saving your money in the form of food and other things you'll need in the future. You can also use the extra money to pay down your debt. If you have credit card debt, chances are it's at a high interest rate (or will be soon when that zero percent introductory rate ends), so it helps you a lot to get rid of that. If you pay off your house sooner then you'll be safer in case you someday lose your job.

You might consider investing some of your surplus cash in a solar energy system. These are getting cheaper all the time, and as of the writing of this book [2020] a solar power system can be had for about the same cost as connecting to the more conventional power mains. When I say "about the same price" I mean to include the time value of money. Depending on your financial circumstances, you might want to use your surplus cash to pay for the whole solar system up front (maybe $10k). Obviously, the first-year cost to you would be very high, but then later years would be almost free. When you consider the entire stream of income from a solar system, the upfront cost ends up being about the same as the value of the discounted stream of electricity.

An added bonus is that you don't pay taxes on this stream of investment income, nor does it become eroded by inflation or NIRP. Even if you don't have the surplus cash to pay for the whole solar energy system up front, you can usually get a loan for the small amount. Then each month you make a payment to the bank rather than to the electric company for your electricity. There are current tax credits available, both federal and state, to help you pay for a home solar energy system, so you should look into that.

**Silver and barter**. You might also want to consider keeping some of your money in the form of silver. For thousands of years, going back to the ancient Greeks and Minoans, silver has been the "poor man's gold". For millions of poor people around the world, silver has been the medium of exchange in many civilizations since before written history. It was only very recently (1964) that silver stopped being a medium of exchange in the United States. Many people will prefer to keep their money in gold, but I'll tell you why I prefer silver.

One gold coin is currently worth about a thousand dozen eggs, but one silver dime is worth about one dozen eggs. Even if the US economy fares very badly, there are still many people who will happily trade you a dozen eggs for a silver dime or 5 pounds of their recently butchered beef for a silver dollar. It could be difficult for someone to make change for a gold coin when people are very poor. Nearly anyone could probably make change for a silver dollar if need be.

Historically, the ratio of the value of gold to silver has been about 16:1, varying between 12:1 and 20:1. However, in the past few years that ratio has gone to over 100:1 because central banks, mostly in China and Russia, have been buying up gold and ignoring silver. These central banks can see the writing on the wall with regard to the coming economic problems in the US and the resulting devaluation of the US dollar. Other countries also are aware that the USD could soon suffer huge losses, but they're bound by loyalty to try to prop up the dollar for as long as possible.

Articles in the financial news always talk about silver being an industrial metal, used in a lot of electronics such as cell phones and computers, and they purposely ignore that it's been a monetary metal for thousands of years. It's my belief that silver will return to being a monetary metal for the vast majority of people, and when that occurs the gold/silver ratio could easily return to the 16:1 or 20:1 range. It's easy to see that silver has a much better upside potential than does gold.

Another possible problem with gold is that it could more easily be stolen by the government. In 1934, the United States had other bad economic problems and the president issued a decree to effectively steal all of the gold from American citizens. It seems shocking, but they really did confiscate gold then immediately devalued the dollar by about 30%. For decades it was actually illegal to own gold in the US, under the threat of a 10 year prison sentence—excluding small amounts of gold such as owning a wedding ring and a necklace). It was only in 1974 that it again became legal to own gold. I consider it unlikely, but the government could again become this tyrannical, or worse. It would be much easier for them to steal peoples' gold than silver, and this risk is another reason why I prefer silver. Some people might disagree with my use of the word "steal" to describe this government action. They buy into the idea that anything that the government does is legal just because they can pass a law, or in this case a Presidential decree. But just making a decree does not make it legal in accordance with the Constitution, which states very clearly that only gold and silver shall be money (not the dubious Federal Reserve Notes). When the government says that you must give up your gold and accept these pieces of paper, and they set the price (to be a bargain for those in power), then it is indeed theft.

You can get silver coins on eBay for close to the price of the silver content if you're patient and pay attention. Don't buy just $1 face value at a time because the shipping charges will be too high of a percentage. Rather, it benefits you to wait until you have enough for $100 face value, which costs around $1,300 at current silver prices. There are various online sites where you can check the current price of silver [40] and the current value of the silver content in US coins made in 1964 or earlier [41]. *Kitco.com* sells bags of $1,000 face value at close to the spot silver price, if you can afford to buy that much a time.

Many people like to collect the 0.999 silver coins made by the US mint, such as the Walking Liberty 1 oz. Coins. Although they're beautiful, I don't like those for a couple of reasons. Since they're nearly pure, they're soft and quickly wear down after moving from hand to hand. They're also easy to tarnish and react with the acids in your skin more than the alloyed coins. I expect a time when silver coins are used as a means of barter between people when the banking system fails and people lose faith in the electronic money. In that case, the soft coins will wear down too quickly, leading many traders to discount their value.

Instead, I prefer the older US coins which were 90% silver and 10% copper. The alloy made them much stronger and more resistant to wear. If you choose to buy silver coins, just go with the common date Roosevelt dimes, Washington quarters and either Kennedy or Franklin halves. Stay away from some of the older ones such as the Standing Liberty quarters (made 1916-1932). Those spent many years in circulation and most of them are worn almost flat (called 'slicks' by collectors). These coins have lost a significant amount of their silver content and might be worth considerably less than the other, less worn, coins.

**Social Security**. You should really consider taking Social Security early. I know that statement would be strongly opposed by government officials and financial advisors. SS is close to not being able to pay all of the retirees the promised benefits and those in the Federal government would prefer that everyone take SS as late as possible, in order to push the problem as far into the future as possible. Financial advisors are afraid to stand out from the crowd, so they won't give you this advice, even if some of them secretly believe it themselves. Let me explain why conventional wisdom is wrong.

The current retirement age for someone born in 1962 is 67. If you choose to take early retirement at 62, then you'll get only 70% of your total monthly benefit. If you do the calculations, then it takes a little less than 16 years until you reach the break-even point between early and normal retirement. But having money early can presumably be invested and make money for you (in normal times, before ZIRP and NIRP), so that means it takes even longer than 16 years to break even between the early/normal retirement.

Financial advisors will say that the average person expects to live until age 79 (a little less for men, more for women). But if you take early retirement at age 62 and it takes 16 years to break even, then you'll be 78 years old, very close to the 79 life expectancy before you show any gain by taking SS at the conventional retirement age. Under these calculations, there's little difference, statistically speaking, of whether you take it early or late. Social Security also offers a little more money for choosing a late retirement at age 70, but the same logic holds that it's about a wash (using these conventional comparisons).

We all like to be optimistic, and most of us believe we'll live a lot longer than average, but do you have any sort of health problems? Maybe you smoke, are overweight, or have high blood pressure, asthma or diabetes? A significant portion, maybe half, of people have one or more of these, and they can be expected to live less than the average age. Then again, you could very well live to be 80, 90, or older. Even so, it makes sense to start collecting your SS money sooner rather than later.

Here's [43] a good video that does a better analysis than I've presented above, including the time value of money (getting money earlier is worth more than getting it later due to interest compounding). In the video, he comes to the conclusion that you would need to live to be about 100 or more in order to get any benefit from the late retirement.

The most important reason to take Social Security early is the political risk. What I mean by this is that our masters in Washington, DC, can choose to change the rules. Never mind that you worked for 30-some years under the old set of rules and have certain expectations. As we discussed in an earlier chapter, it's well-known that SS is in trouble and that eventually something has to be done. Politicians won't work to solve this problem early, meaning they'll all wait until the problem is much bigger and more painful to solve.

Chances are that the changes will be some combination of a reduction in benefits and an increase in taxes. One possible change that's being suggested by some in power is the Universal Basic Income (UBI). This means that everyone, rich and poor, would get a check each month from the government that's meant to cover basic living expenses. $2,000 a month is one number that's been suggested. Of course, this would be paid for by a huge new tax on the middle class, but ignore that for now.

If UBI is implemented, chances are it would take the place of all of the current safety net schemes: welfare, Social Security, disability, unemployment, veteran's benefits and all pensions. One positive thing this has going for it is that it would do away with the vast number of bureaucrats and administrators that are currently needed to watch over the many separate schemes. It would do away with all of the time recipients spend qualifying for unemployment and welfare.

The expense required by hiring literally millions of people to work on these many programs is quite large, so this would streamline the process. Recipients would save much time always having to go to the welfare office or login online in order to prove they still need help. But if you collect SS early as I'm suggesting, then you have the extra years from age 62 until 67 to receive benefits without working. Go ahead, take that 5-year vacation and enjoy life a little before a very uncertain future is upon us.

I consider an increase of the retirement age to be a reduction in benefits, and this is one of the more likely ways that politicians will try to extend the Ponzi scheme that is Social Security. However, if you retire at age 62 and take the lower benefit, they can't claw back the money you've already gotten in benefits. Sure, they can reduce your future benefits along with everyone else's, but they can't take back the checks you've already cashed. If you retire at 62 and the very next day they raise the early retirement to 63, you can't be thrown out. And you won't need to be chasing the horizon that's always moving away from you as they raise the retirement age a little more with each passing year.

A typical way they'll reduce everyone's benefit is to "update" the way they calculate inflation, as they did during the Clinton years, to make the inflation problem appear to be much smaller. This has the dual benefits of making it look like things are rosier than they really are, as well as reducing the cost of living increases for Social Security, veterans' benefits, welfare and other programs.

As discussed earlier, the conventional way of deciding when to retire gives approximately a tie with respect to age 62 or 67. When you have a difficult life choice to make and it seems like a tie, you should try to include other factors in your analysis to find the best decision for you. I think the political risk is a big tie-breaker that swings it strongly in favor of taking the early retirement, but that's just my opinion.

Definitely try to get more education about Social Security and consult other people's opinions. However, if you ask a retirement planner or government worker, they'll always tell you to take SS later. If you ask them about the political risk, they'll either brush it off and say there's no problem, or they'll say "Well, that's entirely unknown so we can't take that into account." Failing to take into account the chance of something doesn't make it go away.

**Internal Exile.** Another thing you can do to help protect yourself and your family is to buy land in the country where it's cheaper. You could also get a trailer to live in if there's no house available and can continue to live cheaply in the trailer or use it while you're building your own home. Today, an acre of land can be bought for as little as $10k.

There's a strong possibility that crime rates will go up when the US starts to crumble. The police will be paid in food, as in Venezuela, and in return the police will mostly spend their time protecting the rich and politically powerful. They already ignore the poor in most respects, so we're halfway there, but this trend will increase. Most of us live in medium to large cities because that's where the higher-paying jobs are; that's where we have to go (or at least think so) in order to support a middle-class lifestyle. But if crime is rampant—theft, robbery, burglary, etc.—you might get fed up with this abuse and want to leave. Maybe you live in an apartment or your house equity is low, so it's worthwhile for you to walk away rather than dealing with the misery of crime, gangs, crushing taxes and open corruption in your city.

I prefer to be as remote as possible in order to stay away from the criminal gangs that are likely to come to dominate the cities. It won't be worthwhile for them to venture too far from their home turf just to go to the target-poor areas of small towns and the country. I prefer the South and West parts of the US (excluding the West Coast), due to the low taxes, good gun laws and nicer climate. Living in the country won't be luxurious, but you might find it is more peaceful and less dangerous than the city or suburbs you left behind.

As food shortages become more and more commonplace, being able to grow your own food gives you more peace of mind. Chickens are easy to raise too. They'll scratch in the dirt and eat insects and plant pieces, as well as table scraps you would otherwise throw away. Eggs are a good source of protein and you can barter those that you don't eat in exchange for your neighbors' milk, butter, pork, beef or vegetables.

There are a lot of people who work from home these days, sometimes called telecommuting or off-site working. Maybe you could do something like that. More companies are moving toward having a large portion of their employees work from home because it saves the company from having to rent office space, as well as paying for electricity, heating and cooling. For example, if you have some computer skills you could build websites for different small companies, or get a job doing programming. Even if you don't already know programming, there are many night courses at community colleges as well as online courses you can take when you have time. Other people work doing telephone support or call-center types of jobs.

If you decide to get a country place, you might find that it's wise to fly below the radar. What I mean is you don't want to draw too much attention or give too much information about yourself. Try to make your house and yard look like your neighbors, something that's typical for the area so you won't stand out. You might also want to consider paying for as much as you can with cash (until cash is made illegal by our masters), because this limits the paper trails. It gives less information to banks and anyone else who wants to snoop in your files.

Learn to use PGP (Pretty Good Privacy) or other strong encryption program. Remember, the Feds can snoop on all your cell phone calls, emails and text messages. You don't really know when they'll give that information to someone to try to use against you. Sure, it's illegal to do this, but will they get caught?

You might consider deleting your Facebook account or at least greatly limiting the information you put on there. Remember, criminals (those in government and the freelancers) like to gather information on their targets. Don't be like the rapper [51] who put pictures of himself and a friend holding a large stack of cash. Then in another video he flashed a picture of his luggage tag which showed his exact address. Then everyone was so surprised when robbers came to his door, shot him dead and took the money.

# Chapter 5
# How to rebuild society from the ashes

====

*"History doesn't repeat itself, but it often rhymes."* - Mark Twain

We've had a good run in the US. We've had an undreamed of rise in prosperity, starting with practically nothing 200 years ago into the single world superpower. We tried our experiment with this huge and all-encompassing nanny state, and it cost us dearly: our standard of living, our influence in the world, and very soon our freedom because we'll have to fight to get it back from the new aristocrats in DC.

Government has been shown to be much less efficient than the market economy at creating prosperity. The empire is ending and it's a bit sad, but we can still be optimistic about the future. One empire dies and a new one is born from the ashes. Greece grew, flourished and eventually died, but not before giving birth to Rome. Rome grew corrupt and withered but gave birth to Old Europe. Old Europe had to go through the Dark Ages where a lot of knowledge was lost, but they had their Renaissance and gave birth to the US (among many other far less successful heirs).

The knowledge and attitudes that made the US great aren't dead (free enterprise, the rule of law, individual rights), but they'll be in remission for awhile. A new Dark Age after we have The Collapse. Where do we go from here? Who will pick up these ideas and grow to become the new leader in human rights, science, the arts, economics and business?

It would be nice if the US only went through a brief Dark Age, but that seems unlikely based on history. England slowly faded away in the

20$^{th}$ century, which is about the best scenario the US could ask for, but I consider this to be unlikely too. England had the US and Europe to fall back on, but the US will have no such help because Europe, Japan, Australia and other democracies are already basket cases.

The simple reason The Collapse will be deep and dark is that people need to suffer a lot before they'll admit they've gone down a wrong path. It's so much easier just to be passive, allow things to get ever-worse and accept the excuses that are provided by our masters. People don't read history and learn from the mistakes of the past (i.e. socialism and tyranny), so they're doomed to repeat the same errors anew with only minor changes.

There's an old quote [60] about Democracy, often attributed to Thomas Jefferson, *"Democracy is nothing more than mob rule, where 51% of the people may take away the rights of the other 49%."*

In the US we started with a constitutional republic, but the protections of the Bill of Rights were gradually eroded by politicians. Some of these politicians were merely cynical and trying to increase their power as much as possible, not caring about damaging the country. They just wanted to get elected one more time and were willing to do anything to get there. Some of them actually thought they were helping.

There's another quote from the great Supreme Court Justice, Louis Brandeis, that applies [61]: *"The greatest dangers to liberty lurk in the insidious encroachment by men of zeal, well-meaning but without understanding."* It doesn't matter so much how we got here, just that we've lost most of the protections from the Bill of Rights.

To rebuild the next free society after this one collapses, we need to look at what we did right and what we did wrong. The Bill of Rights was a great idea, but we need to make each right more explicit so that the power-mad politicians can't subvert things as easily.

For the First Amendment, we need to make it clear that people don't have a fundamental right to not be offended. A lot of mischief and crushing of free speech results from people making laws forbidding you from offending someone. If something is true, then one should be able to say it, and truth should be a valid get-out-of-jail-free defense for any speech crimes.

We also need to make the Second Amendment stronger to prevent the ever chipping away at gun rights. Let's state that the federal and state governments cannot make it unreasonably difficult to buy or own a gun, that taxes on guns cannot be made enormous in an effort to prevent gun ownership, and that guns cannot be taken from someone for mere misdemeanor offenses or unproven accusations.

One way of discouraging Congressmen from creating laws that harm the country is to create a rule in the House and Senate: If anyone sponsors a bill that is then found unconstitutional by the Supreme Court, that Congressman is forbidden to vote for the next month. We also need an explicit law that there shall be nine Supreme Court justice, in order to prevent the President and Senate from conspiring to water down the existing SCOTUS by "packing the court" with many new justices.

**Prevention and roll back.** The Fourth Amendment needs to be strengthened to prevent and roll back the surveillance state that we've become. Add a clause where a warrant has to be obtained from a judge for all spying done on American citizens, and that the citizen will be informed of the warrant and spying within 30 days, or else they're required to file charges against the target for the offense related to the warrant.

This will help make law enforcement take seriously the process of getting warrants. They won't be able to go on so many fishing expeditions and continuously spy on anyone or everyone without having it made public, causing embarrassment to the offending law-enforcement agencies. Of course, the NSA-FBI-CIA will bitterly complain that this will prevent them from getting terrorists, child molesters and drug kingpins. It's doubtful that they can prove this is true, but it should be publicly debated and we should err on the side of freedom.

**Prison reform**. The prohibition against cruel and unusual punishments in the Eighth Amendment should be strengthened to forbid all private prisons. As described earlier, these prisons greatly abuse prisoners by feeding them too little and vastly overcharging for extra food. Politicians and private prison owners work hand-in-hand to get as many prisoners as possible into their system, keep them as long as possible, and milk them of as much money as they can get.

Prisons need far fewer inmates and the focus should be on rehabilitation, not excessive punishment that causes more bitter and psychopathic prisoners to be created out of minor offenders. The use of solitary confinement should be greatly scaled back since studies have shown that it causes insanity and makes prisoners worse, not better. Perhaps allow solitary confinement for at most 2 days and for a maximum of 5% of the prison population at any one time. If a prison uses it more often, then it's clearly engaging in abuse and a federal judge should be able to fire the warden and bring in someone who can meet the guidelines.

We know that we can create a system because plenty of examples exist. All other countries have lower numbers of prisoners per capita and many have lower relapse rates. We need to study what works about those other systems.

**Reform the tax system**. The tax system must be changed so the federal government can take only a certain maximum amount in taxes, say 10% of GDP, down from the current value of about 15% of GDP. This would mean greatly scaling back the ability of politicians to buy votes by way of redistributing vast amounts of wealth.

The tax system should be made more fair to not target the middle class so heavily, but rather spread the tax burden out over even poor people (at a lower and progressive tax rate), in order to prevent the problem of representation without taxation. The level of taxation must be improved in order to allow the US to attract more capital in the future, which in turn allows us to grow. The growth will give us a higher standard of living and allow the US to compete with China, both economically and militarily, in the next 10-30 years.

**Restore transparency in government.** We've seen countless times how the government claimed they had some great reform, and even passed laws to that effect, only to find out much later there was no actual reform. Much of our government is hidden from view. There are many hundreds of billions of dollars being spent that the general public, and nearly all Congressmen, are unaware of. A lot of this money is in so-called "black" (i.e. invisible) programs of the US military as well as the NSA, CIA and FBI. These budgets should be broken down so that at least some top-level numbers are available to the public.

One way we could help restore transparency is to have each of the top three (in terms of national vote totals, not just the usual two suspects) parties name one of their own as an inspector. These three inspectors would have broad powers to demand to see any records and subpoena any witnesses to answer questions under oath. They would have incentive to reveal corruption, waste, fraud and misuse of government money. This setup would also make it so that the largest third party (maybe the Greens or Libertarians) would have some small modicum of power and the ability to reveal corruption and collusion of the other two parties.

Currently, the IRS has the "snitch on your neighbor" rule, whereby you can get a percentage of taxes and penalties if you call their attention to any sort of tax fraud. We need to extend this rule to whistle-blowers who work within the government. They should get cash rewards for helping to reveal the corruption and waste. They should get at least as much protection against reprisals as do other whistle-blowers.

**Justice system.** We need to allow jury nullification of tyrannical laws, and inform juries that they have the right to not only try the facts of the case, but also the law itself. The idea is that a jury can find a defendant not-guilty if they think the law was unjust or that the prosecuting attorney has applied it too harshly against this defendant. This has a rich tradition [54] in the United States and has been used as a backstop to prevent tyranny for hundreds of years, going all the way back to 1670 in England. In the US it's been used to free slaves and acquit people who helped them escape, as well as Vietnam draft evaders and people charged with low-level drug offenses that carry absurdly harsh punishments.

Naturally, courts don't want people to know about this tradition. In fact, if a defense lawyer tells the jury about their right to nullify the law, the lawyer can be punished heavily or disbarred and the case at hand can be declared a mistrial. This shows just how fearful our masters are of the little people having the power to undermine their unjust and tyrannical laws.

**Reform Social Security and the national debt.** It's well known that the Social Security System is unworkable and needs to be greatly reformed. Along with Medicare/Medicaid and interest on the national debt, these 3 things are consuming over half of the US government expenditures every year. We should cancel the debt, and use the money that was formerly used for debt service to be applied to paying SS benefits.

This will be very controversial, and the news will have pictures of widows and orphans owning the bonds and now being penniless. But people have ample warning that the debt will need to be canceled, so that most of the pain will fall on foreign owners of the bonds such as China. This book, among other books and articles, can even be viewed as a warning that the debt will need to be canceled, so if you own these you have ample time to sell them now (near record highs in terms of bond prices).

In effect, China conspired with our corrupt politicians to give them money in exchange for the ability of the Chinese to enslave Americans for generations to come in order to pay the long-term debt. It's exactly the same as the corrupt Chavez and Maduro regimes in Venezuela stealing from the poor people and selling bonds, then stealing the money. Those who colluded to make this collapse happen should be among the first to pay, and repudiating the debt hits them where it hurts.

We can set up rules to make sure that individual small-time investors aren't harmed, up to a maximum of some amount, maybe $200k per person. Perhaps set up a case by case review of who owned the bonds a year before the repudiation. If individuals owned them and were made poor, then return their capital, but not interest accrued.

Obviously, for the US to repudiate the national debt it will make it very difficult or impossible for them to run up huge debts again in the next 50 years (until people forget and the new government proves to investors that it's responsible). The current system encourages nearly unlimited pork-barrel spending because the extra cost can just be added to the national debt. There can be a clause where selling some limited amount of debt is allowed during wartime. This would need to be an actual declaration of war, not one of the fake wars like the War on

Drugs, the War on Poverty or the War on Terrorism (some invisible and ill-defined enemy).

The US needs a balanced budget amendment, which many states already have, in order to force Congress to live within the means of the country and not endanger our future with debt built up to fund pork barrel projects. This would force the difficult decisions to be made immediately between what is truly necessary and what isn't, rather than 20 years later when the problems have become immense and painful.

Here's an interesting positive-feedback loop to consider. If a small but dedicated minority of people starts to call for repudiating the national debt, then buyers of debt will get nervous. They might start buying other assets instead of Treasury bonds. The 10-year bond currently pays around 1%, which is terrible for investors and even less than inflation, but that low interest rate helps make it easier to service that $24 trillion national debt. Even a small amount of default risk can push that 1% up significantly.

But as investors start to lose interest in T-bonds it will push the interest rates up, perhaps to 2%. This doubles the amount it costs to finance the debt, from the current value of 8% [44] of the US budget to 16%. It's not impossible or unheard of for the interest rate to be 2% or even much more. In fact, before the year 2000, the interest rate averaged 6% for a long time, and was 10% for a few years from 1980-1983. It's only a new phenomenon that interest rates are held to 1% or lower. The rate could easily go to 3%, which would cost 24% of the US budget to finance each year. This is a big bite and will surely be paid for the only way the politicians know how: to pile it onto the debt.

Then investors see this rapidly increasing debt and get even shyer about buying treasuries, pushing up interest rates more. Each time around this circle pushes interest rates ever high, worsening the Debt/GDP ratio, and pushing the US closer to having to make the difficult (but crucially necessary) decision to repudiate the debt, increase taxes or decrease spending. We need to come to this juncture in order to bring on The Collapse and therefore be able to start to rebuild something more fair and more competitive in the international economy.

**Break up the new robber barons.** We need to break up the GAF (Google Amazon Facebook) monopolies. We already have precedent for this in the way the oil and railroad monopolies were broken up in the late 1800's and early 1900's. There is currently no political will to harm them because they serve the entrenched politicians, both by direct contributions and by indirect contributions to their causes.

Google also serves politicians by skewing search results. For example, during the 2016 election, they often showed stories against Trump but buried the stories that showed Hillary's illegal email server or other problems. Facebook does the same thing of suppressing some stories and vigorously promoting others, according to what suits their political agenda. YouTube (owned by, Alphabet, the same shell company which owns Google) did their part to help the chosen candidates, including banning or demonetizing many more conservative channels than liberal channels.

You might be a liberal and not care if the GAFs use their kingmaker status to choose Hillary over Trump. But what if they decide to use their ability to elect Joe Biden over Bernie Sanders or Elizabeth Warren? When the US becomes a one-party (i.e. Democrat) state, then this is exactly what they'll be doing, and even as a liberal you should be concerned.

Boss Tweed said "*I don't care who does the voting, so long as I do the nominating.*" In other words, he would nominate both parties' candidates and didn't care which one would win because either way he owned the person in power. This is the same position that the GAFs are in now. Aside from the fact that these huge semi-monopolies can victimize consumers, they also quietly dominate the political process.

We need a return to real competition, and this takes on many facets. We currently have a centralized, top-down kind of approach that comes from Washington, DC. The Soviet Union and other centralized economies have proven time after time that centralized planning is terribly inefficient, and even China has switched to a more decentralized and competition-driven system.

**Reallocate Defense Spending**. An obvious area that needs to be examined is the US defense budget. I'll probably be criticized as unpatriotic by both the Right and Left for even mentioning this, since billions of dollars go to so very many Congressional districts. In the early years of World War II, the Japanese shocked the British by very quickly taking both Hong Kong and Singapore. The British had a very high opinion of their own military strength and even feelings of racial superiority over the Japanese. It turned out to be a huge mistake to underestimate their opponents, as those two fortified cities fell very quickly to the Japanese onslaught. Winston Churchill called the loss of Singapore the biggest defeat ever for the British Empire.

Before the war, there were a few junior officers who had the bravery (or foolish disregard for their careers) to tell their superiors that these colonies were woefully in need of upgraded defenses lest they fall to the Japanese. No one listened to them, and instead accused them of insubordination or lacking faith or lack of patriotism. The same thing could happen to the US.

Here's just one example of many showing how the US needs to improve our defenses and cut the military budget. What comes to mind when you think of a large and proud show of force by the US? Aircraft carriers. Against a small and unsophisticated opponent, maybe North Korea or Libya, the aircraft carrier is a great way to launch fast and unexpected air attacks. They're very useful against these minor players. However, against a large and sophisticated opponent, they would be rapidly destroyed in the first hour of a war or "conflict" as it's likely to be called.

This is the reason the Chinese have only bothered to build two aircraft carriers. And one of those—the Liaoning—is just an old and decrepit Soviet ship that the Russians mothballed because they knew it was useless. The Chinese bought it and spruced it up mostly to use as a show to their own people and as a foreign propaganda piece as if to say, "Observe and tremble at the might of the rising China!"

Perhaps the Chinese even bought one ancient carrier and built another crappy one as a ploy, merely to make the US waste far more money trying to stay ahead in the (non-existent) carrier race. This sort of trick to get the US to waste money on useless defense programs, and therefore deplete more useful programs, has been done before. The Russians used this method as the Backfire Bomber (aka Tupolev-160) in the 1970's and 1980's to trick the US into spending many billions on missiles to counter it, even though its capabilities weren't very good.

The US military industrial complex was happy to blow up the capabilities of this "fearsome" bomber. The media got higher numbers of viewers and the defense companies got billions in new work orders. Everyone was happy, except for the taxpayer who had to pay for the useless military programs.

Since I worked as a missile-guidance engineer for large defense companies for over 30 years I know that the carrier groups can defend against a few incoming missiles, either ballistic or sea-skimming like the Exocet. You might recall that it was a French-made Exocet missile that destroyed the British ship HMS Sheffield in the Falklands war in 1982. Ballistic missiles take a very high (100 miles or more) trajectory, and fly above the atmosphere which makes them extremely fast. But the carrier groups can't defend against a sudden attack of many of these relatively cheap attackers, and the Chinese have thousands of these to use in their coastal batteries. This is the correct and cost-effective response to the US building carriers, and is the reason that China doesn't seriously build up their own fleet of aircraft carriers.

The PLA (People's Liberation Army, effectively the entire armed forces of Red China) could decide to send a message to Washington as well as to test their resolve by rapidly sinking one of these near Taiwan. Using round numbers, a large and modern aircraft carrier like USS Gerald R Ford costs around $14 billion, not counting the value of all of the crew as well as the fighter jets and other equipment. This expensive ship can be sunk with a handful of anti-ship missiles costing around $500k. Even if the PLA spends $10 million on 20 of these missiles, it's still a ratio of over 1000:1 in terms of attrition cost. The Chinese must salivate at the thought of that trade.

It's very likely that a Democratic regime in Washington would quickly abandon many allies (Taiwan, South Korea, Vietnam, Thailand) to avoid being entangled in these "foreign wars", especially after several thousand US crewman are killed. The "peace at any cost" group that pulled the US out of Vietnam 50 years ago is now in power. They don't want protesters opposing any action against China, so the Democrat president would quickly fold.

In this way, the Chinese would be correct that the US was a "paper tiger" (as they frequently call us in their state-run newspapers and television broadcasts). You might be thinking that the Chinese would never dare sink an American aircraft carrier, even if they could, because the US has nuclear weapons. The US has shown a steadfast unwillingness to use nukes in defense, even when North Korea attacked in 1950 and nearly drove the US entirely off the peninsula. The US didn't respond at all more recently when North Korea used a torpedo to sink the ship Cheonan in 2010 [58] because they didn't want to escalate, even using any conventional weapons. So the US would be very unlikely to use nukes to strike back for the sinking of a carrier.

Note that an aircraft carrier doesn't sail alone, but goes with a large convoy of destroyers, missile boats and submarines. But they're still sitting ducks for a significant number of cheap missiles. All of the convoy could quickly come under attack at once, so the cost would not be just the carrier, but quite possibly another 10-20 ships as well. Or maybe the PLA would just send the message by sinking the largest and most visible emblem of American might, the carrier, with the tacit message "We let you off easy this time. Now leave our waters." Either way, it would be a huge embarrassment to the US and would make many allies abandon us in order to quickly make peace with their new Chinese masters.

Rather than allow this to happen, the US needs to stop spending such huge amounts of money on these indefensible targets and spend it in other areas. Specifically, areas where it can actually threaten the Chinese rather than merely acting as targets waiting for their doom.

The above criticism of aircraft carriers is just one example of the gross misappropriation of money in the defense budget that exists merely for show and pork-barrel politics, and isn't useful in the coming altercation. There are many other areas I haven't mentioned where wasteful and ineffective defense spending could be cut, totaling many billions of dollars. Maybe I'll be called unpatriotic for pointing out this weakness, but it needed to be said: the emperor has no clothes.

**Term Limits**. We have term limits on the president, thanks to the Twenty-Second Amendment, but that law didn't go far enough. We still have career politicians on both sides of the aisle that have enormous power and have been there for decades. Incumbent politicians have immense advantages over any challengers. For one, they're well-known due to their free appearances on television. They also have free use of the US mail, which they use to send out newsletters to their constituents, and this too has the effect of making them more well-known which gets them more votes.

Congressmen can also make a lot of money in "speaking fees". This is just a thinly veiled bribe that goes directly into the Congressman's bank account, not his reelection fund. Ostensibly, these fees are supposed to be paid just because Goldman Saks or some other wealthy company is so very interested in what the Congressman has to say, but it's an open secret that it's merely a payoff. Is it any wonder that incumbent Congressmen typically win about 98% of the time in modern elections? And Congress has a terrible approval rating, usually around 72% [59], indicating that most of the public would like to see this changed.

We can fix this situation, but of course Congress has little interest to try. If there are genuine contests for Congressional seats then we won't have these petty tyrants sitting there for most of their lifetimes, enriching themselves and their friends.

**Decentralization and State's Rights**. Ronald Reagan noted that, "*Concentrated power has always been the enemy of liberty.*" Decentralization leads to a more stable system. It's interesting how, when a Democrat is president, the Republican states are the ones urging us to keep state's rights. But when a Republican is president, as we've had since 2016, then it is the most liberal Democratic states like California who are loudly crying for state's rights. We would all be served better if we respected state's rights and moved more power away from the Federal Government and back to the states. The founding fathers were aware of the problem of a centralized government growing too powerful and even put it in writing in the Tenth Amendment.

But over time the Supreme Court of the United States (SCOTUS) has worked to take power away from states and move it to the federal level. It's taken a while, but most constitutional scholars agree that this is the direction power has moved. Remember, the Supreme Court justices are nominated and confirmed based on how well they will "play the game". This means they're chosen for loyalty to a certain party, leading to the justices nearly always voting along party lines in the biggest and most important cases. And both parties agree that the power should move to the Federal Government, so over time the SCOTUS has steadily eroded state's rights and the Tenth Amendment has suffered.

But if we did move back to states having more rights, then most of us would be happier. If California wants to give free healthcare to immigrants, restrict gun rights, legalize marijuana and have higher taxes, then they should be able to do that (within the limits of individual rights, such as respecting the Second Amendment). If Texas wants to have more permissive gun rights, higher speed limits, lower drinking ages and lower taxes (currently having zero income tax, which would horrify the Californians), then they should be allowed this too.

If we have 50 different systems in 50 different states, then the rest of us can look around and see what works. In this way, there would be more competition between states to make a better and happier system within their states. Over time, states will copy some things of other states and we can hope that this leads to a progression of better policies for the whole union. We already have some competition between states with regard to standards of living and taxes. New York has high taxes, and every year many thousands of jobs are lost as businesses and individuals move to low tax states like Texas.

We need more of this competition between state policies, and people will have the ability to vote with their feet, leaving one oppressive state in order to move to one that has the sort of environment they prefer.

Even if some states try some policies that are very counter-productive, like high taxes, they'll lose businesses, lose jobs and lose tax revenue. We should be grateful when these states volunteer to act as bad examples and instruct us on what not to do. Knowing what not to do is as valuable as knowing which things work well. Decentralization allows this kind of experimentation and a gradual evolution toward better policies.

Many young people are rightly angry that they can join the military at 18, or even possibly be drafted in future conflicts and die for their country, but they can't drink a beer on their time off. This is all because the federal government has effectively forced states to adopt 21 as the drinking age. This is an interesting example of federal extortion being used to force states to give up their rights to the federal government, and a sneaky way to get around the Tenth Amendment.

The federal government takes many billions of dollars from the people every year in the form of high taxes. Then the federal government gives money back, for example in the way of highway funding. But, in order to get this large amount of money back that they already paid to the feds, the states are forced to give up their rights and pass a drinking age that is at least 21. Both the far left and the far right loved this law. Usually, when both extremes support something it turns out to be negative for the country and unpopular among the "little people" (so-called by the DC aristocracy).

The hard left loved it because they enjoy social engineering and like to have more and more control of people, getting more people into the legal system and private prisons. The hard right supported raising the drinking age because they would have preferred to make all alcohol illegal. The next best thing is to make the age incrementally higher and higher. Maybe it's age 21 one year and then they raise it to 25 or 30. We get closer and closer to all-out prohibition, and we already know how badly that worked out. It greatly enriched gangsters and led to more violence and more people dying from drinking badly-made and poisoned liquors.

There are plenty of other smaller things that also need to be cleaned up. I haven't delved into the changes needed in the divorce system, the overly-litigious legal system that allows lawyers to sue and make billions of dollars, how the AMA lobbies Congress to reduce the number of people in med school in order to keep out new competition, reforming the public school system to return power to the communities. The whole system of legal foundations is also corrupt, allowing billionaires to move money from one hand to the other hand, and get a big tax write-off by so doing. But they still retain the ability to use the money to do almost anything they deem to benefit humanity, which really means anything that they want. The list of laws and institutions that need change is very long.

# Chapter 6
# Where to shelter from the coming storm?

———

———

IN CHAPTER 4 I TALKED about how to mitigate the pain to yourself and your family when the US economy goes down. I suggested getting a country place so you'd have somewhere to go if the cities became too horrible. Getting a country home can be considered to be a form of internal exile. In some circumstances though you might want to leave the US entirely for a few years during the worst and most tyrannical times to come.

In this chapter I talk about some foreign countries where you can live reasonably comfortably and cheaply. Everywhere has its problems and none of these places are perfect, but they might make a good refuge for a while. I could offer a lot of information on Thailand and the Philippines since I've lived in both countries, but I'll just touch on a few of the different pros and cons. If you are serious about going abroad, then I suggest reading many websites and watching a lot of Youtube videos to educate yourself. It is important for you to be exposed to many different points of view so that you can make a good decision, and all of the many details are beyond the scope of this book.

**Thailand:** In 2018, I lived in Chiang Mai, Thailand, for 6 months and enjoyed it. The people are friendly and the cost of living is low compared to most of the US. It's hot and humid, as you would expect for a tropical area, a lot like Florida in the US. If you're tired of the cold winters in the Northeast or Midwest parts of the US, this might be a good choice for you. While I was there I didn't own or rent a car, but used Grab (a taxi service like Uber or Lyft) and it worked well. You can get around town for $2 for a few miles, or about $3-4 to go all the way across town. There are buses for cheap prices if you want to go to other nearby towns, and you can ride the overnight train to Bangkok. It's only $25 per person for a private carriage for 2 people for this 12 hour ride.

While I was in Chiang Mai during 2018, I had nasal surgery. Before the surgery, I had a thorough group of diagnostics that included a chest x-ray, EKG, CT scan, multiple blood tests and 6-7 doctor's exams, before and after the procedure. For the recovery I had a huge private room on the $11^{th}$ floor of the hospital, with a bed, two couches, a TV, fridge, microwave, table and chairs. I spent three days in this room and had many doctor and nurse visits during that time. The total cost was about $2500. This is about $1/10^{th}$ of the $25,000 that I've paid for the same thing in the US, except the latter was on an outpatient basis with far fewer doctor's visits or diagnostics.

Now, I know what you're thinking: is it safe? Most Thai doctors have been trained in either the US or Western Europe and seem every conscientious. They speak English very well, having spent so many years studying abroad. All in all, I'd say that the quality in Thailand was quite a bit better than in the US and as I mentioned earlier, the price is far less. This just illustrates how the cost of healthcare in the US has been driven absurdly high by our over-regulation and the overly-litigious legal system.

The above description of healthcare in Thailand brings up my own personal strategy toward affordable healthcare. When you consider the conventional way to do healthcare in the US, you pay about $1500/month for health insurance ($18k per year) plus you pay about $5k for your deductible, plus you pay various doctor co-pays and co-insurance (maybe 10-20% of the cost). When you add all of these up, you could end up paying at least $25,000 per year.

I look at my own healthcare as being divided into three tiers. I don't carry health insurance so I avoid that $25k per year. In the first tier I have various small things like an earache, vaccinations or seeing an allergist. I just pay for all of these out of pocket. That $25,000 per year I saved goes a long way toward all of these little things, and doctors are very happy to learn that you're paying cash. For the second tier of my healthcare I consider medium sized things such as the sinus surgery ($2500 as described above), having pre-cancerous moles removed and other things. For this second tier I go to Thailand or some other advanced yet cheap place to get these things done. And finally, my third tier is for the really big things: a heart attack, cancer or an organ transplant.

Let's be realistic here, these third tier things are going to wipe out almost anyone in the middle class. You have to pay your 10-20% coinsurance every year on these things, and every year you pay the $5k-$10k of deductible since something major like this is likely to stretch out into years of medical treatments. Even 10% of a $5 million bill is half a million dollars, which probably eats up most of your nest egg.

My strategy for this third tier is to just become a ward of the state in the US. They'll still do the surgery, and yes it will wipe me out financially, but I would be wiped out anyway even if I had carried insurance for all of those years. But if I never have a huge thing happen, then I come out far ahead by not having health insurance and paying for all of the small and medium things on my own. Obamacare has made health insurance so very expensive for most of us in the middle class when you include all of the costs described above, that it no longer makes financial sense for me to carry it. Of course your results may vary, based on your economic and health circumstances, but I urge you to think outside the box and consider your alternatives.

Thailand does have some things that aren't perfect, as you would expect. The country is ruled by a military dictatorship. From time to time there are protesters calling for more Democracy. The ruling junta more or less tolerates these, though sometimes there is fighting between the police and the protesters. As a foreigner, you should stay away from these and try not to take sides. You're a guest in their country and it's not your place to change the government, even though you probably have your preferences. The current arrangement seems fairly stable and peaceful, so it's a nice place to live.

Another thing that bothered me a little bit about Thailand was the racism. In the US, especially among the left, racism is the biggest form of evil. In fact, it's pretty much the only thing they stand for and everything comes back to racism for them. But in much of the world, racism is the norm. It's common for unworldly people everywhere to consider themselves the best in the world, or God's chosen people. In China you'll be called a "*gweilo*", which roughly means "foreign devil". In Israel they have Zionism. In Japan you'll be a "*gaijin*", and in Korea they're also very aware of who is their countryman and who's an outsider.

The idea of saying "our group is better" is very common in the world. If you extend the idea of racism to any kind of groupism, you'll be able to see that the Democratic Party frequently engages in this same practice, despite their much-advertised tolerance or inclusiveness. For example, Hillary labeled Trump supporters as "deplorables" [86] and Obama labeled mid-westerners bitter and said that they "cling to guns and religion" [87]. All of these sorts of things are meant to appeal to the Democratic base who like to view themselves as superior and, ironically, so much more tolerant.

The name-calling isn't tolerant, but it's overlooked. Democrats love to point out how they support gay marriage and are so very accepting of alternate lifestyles, but when you ask them about 3-party marriage they give a horrified look and respond with something like, "No! That's something Mormon's do. They're hardcore Christians and we hate them." So you can see that, even among the US political aristocracy, it's very common to say how superior your group is and having a blind spot toward your own intolerance.

It's no surprise that racism is alive in Thailand too, where you'll be called a *"farang"*, which means something like "foreigner" and carries the connotation that you're a bit inferior. You'll have to get used to it. As I said, it's a bit annoying but they're just going along with the propaganda they've learned their entire lives, calling you by the label that everyone else calls you.

I'm not meaning to downplay racism, but as I said it's pretty much the norm throughout the world. In the US, I'm more afraid of the people who want to burn witches, than I am of the witches themselves. I'm more afraid of the people like ANTIFA who see racists in every office and every home and want to violently attack them. In Thailand, while they might be racist they won't overtly attack you.

One area that might irk you is the tradition of "one price Thai, one price *farang*". Meaning, you'll pay more for the exact same thing than a Thai would pay. If you go to a temple, they have an admission price which might be $2 for Thais and $7 for *farangs*. Okay, I halfway understand this because the temples are supported by the government, which means that the people pay their taxes to keep up the temples. Those notions of separation of church and state have no place here. Since the people pay taxes then it makes sense that they'd get a cheaper entrance fee than foreigners, sort of.

You'll see the dual pricing elsewhere too. If you go to a buffet they expect you to eat everything on your plate. There's a sign on the wall saying, in both English and Thai, that you'll pay an extra charge if you have wastage. But you'll notice that the one in the Thai language lists a price of about $1 while the one in English charges an extra $3. It's just the way they are.

Another area where this racism will come up in Thailand, and can be very expensive for you, is if you are in a traffic accident. You'll quickly find that it's always the foreign person's fault. Even if it's not your fault, the court will certainly find that it was indeed your fault. Part of the problem is that the judges are appointed and if a judge ever ruled in favor a dirty farang and against a Thai, there would be hell to pay. It just won't happen. My advice is to just pay the $2 and ride a Grab taxi rather than renting a motorbike or a car. Another reason to let someone else do the driving is that Thai roads are among the most dangerous in the world. People drive very close together and there are a lot of accidents, and since you don't know the customs that puts you even more at risk than the natives.

**Philippines:** In 2020 I spent 3 months in Cebu, Philippines, and enjoyed it as much as I enjoyed Thailand. It's a bit cheaper than Thailand. For example, transportation is very cheap. There are motorized tricycles, rather like a motorcycle with a covered sidecar, and these cost 8 pisos (about 16 cents US) to go a couple of miles. They carry around 5-6 people, so don't be surprised if you're packed against another person, or you have to ride on the back of the motorcycle behind the driver.

The Filipino medical system is similar to that of Thailand: high quality and very low priced compared to the US. They claim to be democratic and the people do vote, but it seems to me that the system is really very similar to the military junta in Thailand, where people can be locked up without any trial or charges, and dissent is sometimes harshly put down. This is typical throughout the world, and in fact the US is going toward this too, where the written law is quite different from the law as it really is.

One aspect of the Philippines that I prefer is the immigration system. In Thailand you have to keep going back every 28 days to get an updated visa, and it takes maybe 4-6 hours of sitting around the office with a hundred other foreign people waiting for your turn. Then after you're in Thailand for 56 days, you're required to leave the country then come back in. Many people ride a bus across the border to Laos, Myanmar, or Cambodia then come back all in the same day. It's a big pain though, wasting a lot of time and money. It's almost as though Thailand is trying more for the sex tourists who want to stay just a week or two, spend a lot of money then go home. They make it difficult and expensive for people who want to stay for a long time such as a year or two.

Thailand does have a retirement visa that allows you to stay long term and check in with immigration every 6 months, but it is difficult to get. The bureaucracy surrounding it is complex and some of the rules are even contradictory. For example, one of the many requirements is that you should have about $20,000 in a Thai bank before you apply for the retirement visa. I went to 6 different banks trying to open an account and at every bank they told me the same thing: I first had to get the retirement visa, or a work visa. As you can see, it's a chicken and egg thing: you need to open a bank account before you get the retirement visa, but you first need to get the retirement visa before the bank account. I've heard that you could bribe someone to have the bank open an account for you and overlook that you don't yet have the retirement visa, so maybe the bribery is the only way to work the system.

The Filipino immigration is easier though. You get one month the first time and then later two months and then six months on your visa. This means you don't have to go to the immigration office nearly as often. The Filipino immigration office is also much less crowded. I've been in and out of there several times in about 20-30 minutes. And in the Philippines they don't make you leave the country every 56 days as they in Thailand.

You might also like that everyone in the Philippines speaks English. The US beat Spain in the Spanish-American war in 1898 and obtained the Philippines and Cuba. The Philippines were a US colony for about 50 years, and then soon after WWII they became their own country. Before the US took over, there were (and still are) something like 186 local languages for the people who are spread out over around 7000 different islands. It seems that every large or medium sized island and every town has their own language. Since everyone in government spoke English during the American colonial period, it was much more convenient for them to agree on using this one language rather than any single language of a small group. They've continued to use English in government to this day.

Tagalog is the local language spoken in their capital and largest city, Manila, and this serves as a kind of standard too, with many TV shows and popular songs in this language. But everyone learns English throughout their schooling and it will be easy for you to communicate there. The Filipino people seem very intelligent to me. For example, nearly every person speaks at least 3 languages: their local language, English and Tagalog. In the US, some people speak 2 languages (typically English and Spanish) but only a small percentage speaks 3 or more languages.

There are several other countries you might want to consider moving to for a year or two. Costa Rica is fairly peaceful and they're quite a bit closer to the US than the Asian countries I mentioned earlier. Ecuador is inexpensive, with a good healthcare system. They also accept US dollars, saving you money on the currency conversions as well as making it easier for you to mentally figure out if something is a good price. You might remember that Ecuador was the country that shielded Wikileaks founder Julian Assange from extradition to the US. For those 7 years that he stayed in the Ecuadoran embassy in London, between 2012-2019. Ecuador eventually caved in to US pressure and turned him over to the British police, but you might like the fact that Ecuador is (sometimes) not afraid to go their own way, independent of too much US influence.

Before you choose any of these countries I'd recommend reading a lot of personal experience stories online and watching many YouTube videos to learn about the culture and how much it will cost you to live there comfortably.

**Other possibilities.** There are other groups talking about building oil-platform types of installations in international waters to have their own country, rather like the Principality of Sealand [90]. It seems risky, both from pirates and jealous governments, but maybe it would be your cup of tea. Here's a story [88] about a couple who made a lot of money in Bitcoin and then used that to make a floating home in international waters a little over 12 miles offshore from Thailand. The Thai government eventually raided them, and now they could get the death penalty. This example highlights just how weak international law is. There's no real international police force or international court that you could rely on for justice, despite the fact that the US and UN both sometimes pose as such. And if a country's military decides to attack you, even if you're in international waters, you don't really have any recourse.

Maybe you could play the situation off between two competing large powers, such as between US and China, so that neither would want to kill you for fear of the other one blowing up the incident to cause international embarrassment. This is where we are now: your rights can be easily violated and you rely on social media to spread the story and cause someone embarrassment. It's only the court of public opinion that helps you keep some tiny part of your rights, and the same thing happens in the US. People sometimes use their smartphones to take video recordings of corrupt police beating people for little or no reason. If no one else is around, oftentimes these police will confiscate the phones of the few bystanders, erase video or just crush the phone beneath their heel for "interfering with police work". It's their word against yours, and in a police state the government will always side with the police.

Another possibility for internal exile (or "internet exile") is to continue to live in the US, but to spend most of your time and energy in an online world. This possibility was examined in the dystopian novel *Ready Player One*, where people in the US live in poverty and pollution, but they spend most of their time in an enormous and richly detailed online game called OASIS. In this game, they attend school, make friends, socialize and find entertainment. To me this seems like a rather sad and meager existence, but is still a possibility that some people will choose.

Already we have many young people in the US who have given up on getting a job or a life partner and spend their time living with their parents playing World of Warcraft (WOW) or other video game for 12-14 hours a day. Japan has many similar people whom they call "*hikikomori*". Perhaps as the economy continues to deteriorate, more people will withdraw from the real world and live this way.

# In Closing

THROUGHOUT THIS BOOK I've tried to show how the US is already moving backwards in many key areas compared to other advanced countries, though the government cheerleaders will tell you that everything is wonderful. They'll point to their carefully gamed statistics and call on their academic henchmen to justify their antisocial and destructive behavior. I've shown the causes and alerted you to the fake causes that the billionaire-owned mainstream media will blame over and over.

I've described how it will unfold as the US becomes a one-party state, dissolves individual rights, punishes investment and drives out capital, leading the country to overall poverty and eventually to hunger. And I've described how you can mitigate the misery that you and your family have to endure by, for example, finding a place to live far out in the country, away from the cities, and making yourself less of a target as you fly below the radar of thieves. There's much more to learn and I encourage you to look at the books that I've mentioned to see more detail about how The Collapse is likely to occur.

# Afterword

MOST OF THIS BOOK WAS written before the Covid-19 virus and so I haven't included the resulting changes. I would have commented on the huge pork barrel "stimulus" programs. These bi-partisan bills were just shameful packages of mostly wasteful and unrelated spending. Even though they gave $1,200 to each taxpayer as a kind of sop, they also gave many billions (or about $4 trillion so far) to large corporations. These corporations should have just gone broke, been bought out by better management teams, and then gone on to serve the public better.

I've taken well-meaning criticism from friends who have said that my book unfairly targets Democrats for most of the blame. I'll say that there's plenty of blame to go around, and Republicans have also participated in a great many of the problems that have befallen the country. But when you're top dog everyone talks about you, for better or worse.

When people criticize fast food for having too much fat, too much salt, and too little vitamins, they invariably bring up McDonald's. It's not that McDonald's is any worse than Wendy's, Taco Bell or Burger King. They're simply top dog and they get to stand in as a symbol for the others.

Democrats should feel proud that they're the dominant party in US politics, and as mentioned throughout these pages they'll soon be the leaders of the single party state. This makes them and their leadership, like Hillary Clinton, Barak Obama and Nancy Pelosi, fair game. They're not the only members of our corrupt aristocracy and this book was not meant to give a complete accounting.

# Citations

——

[1] SOMETIMES ASCRIBED to Nietzsche: "If you want to know what the average person will do in any particular situation, find the one thing that requires the least amount of thought."

[2] "CDC Data Show U.S. Life Expectancy Continues to Decline" American Academy of Family Physicians, December 10, 2018

https://www.aafp.org/news/health-of-the-public/
20181210lifeexpectdrop.html

[3] "Rankings: Living standards" The Economist

https://worldinfigures.com/rankings/topic/9

[4a] "For most U.S. workers, real wages have barely budged in decades" Pew Research Center, Washington, D.C., August 7, 2018

https://www.pewresearch.org/fact-tank/2018/08/07/
for-most-us-workers-real-wages-have-barely-budged-for-decades/

[4b] Shadow Government Statistics: Analysis Behind and Beyond Government Economic Reporting

http://www.shadowstats.com/

[4c] "Historical Home Prices: Monthly Median Value in the US from 1953-2019", DQYDJ, October 3, 2019

https://dqydj.com/historical-home-prices/

[4e] "The National Debt Explained", Investopedia, Apr 13, 2020

https://www.investopedia.com/updates/usa-national-debt/

[5] U.S Bureau of Labor Statistics, Washington, DC

https://www.bls.gov/

[6] Shadow Government Statistics: Analysis Behind and Beyond Government Economic Reporting

http://www.shadowstats.com/

[7] "Index details: Data of press freedom ranking 2020", RSF Reporters Without Borders

https://rsf.org/en/ranking_table

[8] "Corporate Income Tax Rates around the World, 2016", Tax Foundation, August 18, 2016

https://taxfoundation.org/
corporate-income-tax-rates-around-world-2016/

"List of Countries by Corporate Tax Rate", Trading Economics,

https://tradingeconomics.com/country-list/corporate-tax-rate

[9] "60 of America's biggest companies paid no federal income tax in 2018", CBS News, April 12, 2019

https://www.cbsnews.com/news/
2018-taxes-some-of-americas-biggest-companies-paid-little-to-no-federal-ir

"Amazon paid a 1.2% tax rate on $13,285,000,000 in profit for 2019", Yahoo! Finance, February 5, 2020

https://finance.yahoo.com/news/
amazon-paid-a-12-tax-rate-on-13285000000-in-profit-for-2019-21084792

[10] "Jeff Bezos Just Made a $10 Million Political Donation. Here's Where the World's Richest Man Is Putting His Money", Money, September 5, 2018

https://money.com/
jeff-bezos-just-made-a-10-million-political-donation-heres-where-the-worlds-r

"The politics of Jeff Bezos", The Washington Post, August 7, 2013

https://www.washingtonpost.com/news/the-fix/wp/2013/08/07/
the-politics-of-jeff-bezos/

"Meet the Millionaires Bankrolling The Election", Vanity Fair, October 24, 2016

https://www.vanityfair.com/news/2016/10/
meet-the-billionaires-bankrolling-the-presidential-election

"Trump Leak Now Points To Bezos' Hidden $600M Deal With Obama CIA To Feed Washington Post", Conservative Daily Post, February 24, 2017

https://conservativedailypost.com/
trump-leak-now-points-to-bezos-hidden-600m-deal-with-obama-cia-to-feed-w

"WIKILEAKS: Zuckerberg Colluded with Hillary Clinton Campaign", The Black Sphere, September 29, 2017

https://theblacksphere.net/2017/09/
zuckerberg-colluded-with-hillary-clinton-with-hillary-clinton-campaign/

"Mark Zuckerberg sought advice from Clinton campaign via Sheryl Sandberg about getting involved in politics, leaked documents reveals", Daily Mail, October 19, 2016

https://www.dailymail.co.uk/news/article-3850930/
Mark-Zuckerberg-sought-advice-Clinton-campaign-Sheryl-Sandberg-getti

[11] "Google and Facebook Tighten Grip on US Digital Ad Market", eMarketer, September 21, 2017

https://www.emarketer.com/Article/
Google-Facebook-Tighten-Grip-on-US-Digital-Ad-Market/1016494

[12] "Amazon's share of the US e-commerce market is now 49%, or 5% of all retail spend", Tech Crunch, July 13, 2018

https://techcrunch.com/2018/07/13/
amazons-share-of-the-us-e-commerce-market-is-now-49-or-5-of-all-retail-s

[13] "Kanehiro Takaki and the control of beriberi in the Japanese Navy", JRSM, August 2013

https://www.ncbi.nlm.nih.gov/pmc/articles/PMC3725862/

[14] "A Tough Road: Cost To Develop One New Drug Is $2.6 Billion; Approval Rate for Drugs Entering Clinical Development is Less Than 12%", Policy & Medicine, March 21, 2019

https://www.policymed.com/2014/12/
a-tough-road-cost-to-develop-one-new-drug-is-26-billion-approval-rate-fo

[15] "Germany's Rich Herbal Traditions", Mother Earth Living, September 2004

https://www.motherearthliving.com/mother-earth-living/
germanys-rich-herbal-traditions

[16a] "How U.S. Healthcare Costs Compare to Other Countries", Investopedia, January 7, 2020

https://www.investopedia.com/articles/personal-finance/072116/
us-healthcare-costs-compared-other-countries.asp

[16b] "How does health spending in the U.S. compare to other countries?", Health System Tracker, December 7, 2018

https://www.healthsystemtracker.org/chart-collection/
health-spending-u-s-compare-countries/#item-average-wealthy-countries-spen

[16c] "Estimated annual percentage change in medical costs in the United States from 2007 to 2020", Statista, September 19, 2019

https://www.statista.com/statistics/720767/
medical-cost-trend-in-us/

[17] "U.S. education spending tops global list, study shows", CBS News, June 25, 2013

https://www.cbsnews.com/news/
us-education-spending-tops-global-list-study-shows/

[18] "U.S. students' academic achievement still lags that of their peers in many other countries", Pew Research Center, February 15, 2017

https://www.pewresearch.org/fact-tank/2017/02/15/
u-s-students-internationally-math-science/

[19] "Incarceration Rates By Country 2020", World Population Review

https://worldpopulationreview.com/countries/
incarceration-rates-by-country/

[20a] "Incarceration Rates By Country 2020", World Population Review

https://worldpopulationreview.com/countries/
incarceration-rates-by-country/

[20b] "Recidivism in the Unites States - An Overview", Atlas Corps,
May 31, 2017

https://atlascorps.org/recidivism-united-states-overview/

[21a] "Audit: private prisons cost more than state-run prisons", The
Associated Press, January 1, 2019

https://apnews.com/af7177d9cce540ab9f2d873b99437154

[21b] "Private Prison Contracts and Minimum Occupancy Clauses",
American University Business Law Review, November 19, 2017

http://www.aublr.org/2017/11/
private-prison-contracts-minimum-occupancy-clauses/

[22] "Maggots With a Side of Dirt? What Privatization Does to Prison
Food", Governing, February 1, 2018

https://www.governing.com/topics/public-justice-safety/
gov-private-food-service-prisons-aramark-trinity-ohio-michigan.html

[23] "For-profit Prisons", OpenSecrets

https://www.opensecrets.org/industries/indus.php?ind=G7000

[24] "Joe Biden Starts Presidential Campaign By Praising Antifa", Daily
Caller, April 25, 2019

https://dailycaller.com/2019/04/25/joe-biden-antifa/

"Joe Biden Called Domestic Terrorist Group Antifa "Courageous" In
His 2020 Announcement, RedState, April 25, 2019

https://www.redstate.com/brandon_morse/2019/04/25/
joe-biden-kicks-off-2020-campaign-calling-antifa-courageous/

[25] NA

[26] "U.S. Births Fell To A 32-Year Low In 2018; CDC Says Birthrate Is In Record Slump", NPR, May 15, 2019

https://www.npr.org/2019/05/15/723518379/
u-s-births-fell-to-a-32-year-low-in-2018-cdc-says-birthrate-is-at-record-level

[27] "Remembering Nixon's Wage and Price Controls", CATO Institute, August 16, 2011

https://www.cato.org/publications/commentary/
remembering-nixons-wage-price-controls

[28] "How Roman Central Planners Destroyed Their Economy", Foundation for Economic Education, October 5, 2016

https://fee.org/articles/
how-roman-central-planners-destroyed-their-economy/

[29] NA

[30] "Politics is the art of looking for trouble, finding it everywhere, diagnosing it incorrectly and applying the wrong remedies." - Groucho Marx, AZ Quotes

https://www.azquotes.com/quote/189277

[31] "More than 44% of Americans pay no federal income tax", Market Watch, February 26, 2019

https://www.marketwatch.com/story/
81-million-americans-wont-pay-any-federal-income-taxes-this-year-heres-why-

[32] "Life expectancy at birth, total (years) - Russian Federation", The World Bank

https://data.worldbank.org/indicator/
SP.DYN.LE00.IN?end=2010&locations=RU&start=1986

[33] "Cyprus, Greece and Beyond: The "Bail-in" and Confiscation of Bank Deposits: The Birth of the New Financial Order", Global Research, July 8, 2015

https://www.globalresearch.ca/
bail-in-the-birth-of-the-new-financial-order/5330946

[34] "The problem with socialism is that you eventually run out of other people's money." - Margaret Thatcher, GoodReads

https://www.goodreads.com/quotes/
138248-the-problem-with-socialism-is-that-you-eventually-run-out

[35] "UK: National Health Service to Deny Treatment for 'Racist or Sexist Language, Gestures, Behaviour'", Breitbart, November 4, 2019

https://www.breitbart.com/europe/2019/11/04/
uk-national-health-service-to-deny-treatment-for-racist-or-sexist-language-g

[36] "State Fiscal Rankings", Mercatus Center at George Mason University, October 9, 2018

https://www.mercatus.org/publications/urban-economics/
state-fiscal-rankings

[37] "Everybody has a plan until they get punched in the mouth." - Mike Tyson, Brainy Quotes

https://www.brainyquote.com/quotes/mike_tyson_382439

[38] (In 2012 Exxon made $44.9 billion) United States Securities and Exchange Commission

https://www.sec.gov/Archives/edgar/data/34088/000003408813000011/xom10k2012.htm

[39] "Alphabet reports Q4 2019 revenue of $46.07 billion, $15B/year YouTube ad revenue", 9 to 5 Google, February 3, 2020

https://9to5google.com/2020/02/03/alphabet-q4-2019-earnings/

[40] https://www.kitco.com/

[41] "U.S. Circulated Silver Coins", Coinflation

http://www.coinflation.com/silver_coin_values.html

[42] "Average U.S. Retirement Age Rises to 62", Gallup, April 28, 2014

https://news.gallup.com/poll/168707/average-retirement-age-rises.aspx

"What Is the Average Age of Retirement in the US?", Retire in Style, March 4, 2020

https://www.retireinstyleblog.com/average-age-retirement-in-us/

[43] "Best age to collect Social Security. Should I collect now or later?"

https://www.youtube.com/watch?v=9Gy1_LCWXiI

[44] "Policy Basics: Where Do Our Federal Tax Dollars Go?", Center on Budget and Policy Priorities, April 9, 2020

https://www.cbpp.org/research/federal-budget/policy-basics-where-do-our-federal-tax-dollars-go

[45] "The Stunning Statistical Fraud Behind The Global Warming Scare", Investor's Business Daily, March 29, 2018 (Although I'm not a fan of editorials, this is a good piece.)

https://www.investors.com/politics/editorials/
the-stunning-statistical-fraud-behind-the-global-warming-scare/

[46] "Confirmed: FBI Was Spying on the Trump Campaign", Townhall, May 18, 2018

https://townhall.com/tipsheet/katiepavlich/2018/05/18/
confirmed-the-fbi-was-spying-on-the-trump-campaign-and-used-wiretaps-

[47] "The Reckoning of Morris Dees and the Southern Poverty Law Center", The New Yorker, March 21, 2019

https://www.newyorker.com/news/news-desk/
the-reckoning-of-morris-dees-and-the-southern-poverty-law-center

[48] "Clinton Foundation Scandal", Investor's Business Daily, March 7, 2018

https://www.investors.com/politics/clinton-foundation-scandal/

[49] "Obama presents NSA reforms with plan to end government storage of call data", The Guardian, January 17, 2014

https://www.theguardian.com/world/2014/jan/17/
obama-nsa-reforms-end-storage-americans-call-data

[50] "Barack Obama Signs 'USA Freedom Act' to Reform NSA Surveillance", NBC News, June 3, 2013

https://www.nbcnews.com/storyline/nsa-snooping/
senate-vote-measure-reform-nsa-surveillance-n368341

[51] "Pop Smoke Dead, Murdered in Home Invasion Robbery", TMZ, February 19, 2020

https://www.youtube.com/watch?v=qfATGLIGeM8

[52] Rand, Ayn. "For the New Intellectual", 1961.

[53] "NASA's "Global Cooling" Announcement Destroys Global Warming Hoax", The Millennium Report, January 30, 2019

http://themillenniumreport.com/2019/01/
nasas-global-cooling-announcement-destroys-global-warming-hoax/

[54] "It's Perfectly Constitutional to Talk About Jury Nullification", American Civil Liberties Union, January 22, 2019

https://www.aclu.org/blog/free-speech/
its-perfectly-constitutional-talk-about-jury-nullification

[55] "Heretical Thoughts About Science and Society" - Essay by Freeman Dyson, Edge, August 7, 2007

https://www.edge.org/3rd_culture/dysonf07/dysonf07_index.html

[56] "Al Gore: We Need to 'Punish Climate Change Deniers'", The Washington Sentinel, March 17, 2015

https://thewashingtonsentinel.com/
al-gore-we-need-to-punish-climate-change-deniers/

[57] "David Stockman on the Coming Financial Panic and the 2020 Election", LewRockwell.com, September 14, 2019

https://www.lewrockwell.com/2019/09/david-stockman/
david-stockman-on-the-coming-financial-panic-and-the-2020-election/

[58] "North Korea: 'No apology' for S Korea Cheonan sinking", BBC New, March 24, 2015

https://www.bbc.com/news/world-asia-32013750

[59] "U.S. Congress - public approval rating 2019-2020", Statista, April 30, 2020

https://www.statista.com/statistics/207579/
public-approval-rating-of-the-us-congress/

[60] "Democracy is nothing more than mob rule, where 51% of the people may take away the rights of the other 49%." Thomas Jefferson

https://www.monticello.org/site/research-and-collections/
democracy-nothing-more-mob-rulespurious-quotation

[61] "The greatest dangers to liberty lurk in the insidious encroachment by men of zeal, well meaning but without understanding."- Brandeis, Louis, L., Supreme Court justice.

https://www.brainyquote.com/quotes/louis_d_brandeis_169458

[62] "The high suicide rate among those who tangle with the Clintons", Patriot Retort, July 15, 2017

http://patriotretort.com/high-suicide-rate-among-tangle-clintons/

[63] "Not One Democratic Presidential Candidate Responds to Question Asking Them if They Condemn Antifa", CNS News, August 8, 2019

https://www.cnsnews.com/news/article/mark-jennings/
not-one-democratic-presidential-candidate-will-condemn-violence-riddled

[64] "Left-Wing Rioters Attack Trump Supporters Leaving Minneapolis Rally", Breitbart, October 10, 2019

https://www.breitbart.com/2020-election/2019/10/10/
left-wing-rioters-attack-trump-supporters-leaving-minneapolis-rally/

[65] Firesign Theater, "Shoes for the dead". This story is fictional, a joke to make fun of the current political system of doing favors and wasting taxpayer money, but the dynamic is correct and closely parallels how the system works in the US.

http://firesigntheatre.com/media/media.php?item=sfi-tl

[66] "How Much Does It Cost to Become President?", Investopedia, January 31, 2020

https://www.investopedia.com/insights/cost-of-becoming-president/

[67] "Facts are stubborn things" (Global warming supporters claim that rising lake levels and falling lake levels both support the theory.), Dr. John Robson, October 29, 2019

https://www.youtube.com/watch?v=bGxDqUmW6z0.

[68] "Believe only half of what you see and nothing that you hear." - Edgar Allan Poe

https://www.azquotes.com/author/11738-Edgar_Allan_Poe

[69] "If you feel safe in the area you're working in, you're not working in the right area. Always go a little further into the water than you feel you're capable of being in. Go a little bit out of your depth. And when you don't feel that your feet are quite touching the bottom, you're just about in the right place to do something exciting." - David Bowie

https://www.azquotes.com/author/1736-David_Bowie

[71] Henley, Don, "In the Garden of Allah", song, 1995.

[72] "U.S. students' academic achievement still lags that of their peers in many other countries", Pew Research Center, February 15, 2017

https://www.pewresearch.org/fact-tank/2017/02/15/
u-s-students-internationally-math-science/

[73] "On some great and glorious day the plain folks of the land will reach their heart's desire at last, and the White House will be adorned by a downright moron." - H.L. Mencken

https://www.azquotes.com/author/9962-H_L_Mencken

[74] "China – The First Artificial Intelligence Superpower", Forbes, January 14, 2020

https://www.forbes.com/sites/cognitiveworld/2020/01/14/
china-artificial-intelligence-superpower/#26501f792f05[1]

[75] "It's Getting Harder to Spot a Deep Fake Video", Bloomberg, September 27, 2018

https://www.youtube.com/watch?v=gLoI9hAX9dw

[76] MPFC_S02E06 (ep.19) It's A Living (or School Prizes) "Election Night Special" (Monty Python reference to the Silly Party and the Very Silly Party.)

https://www.youtube.com/watch?v=7Xm_TRekjno

[77] "Obama – If You Like Your Healthcare Montage", CNN, July 21, 2016

https://www.youtube.com/watch?v=44kyHOPEZV8

[78] "The Quantum Gap with China", FP, November 28, 2017

1. https://www.forbes.com/sites/cognitiveworld/2020/01/14/
china-artificial-intelligence-superpower/#a5c02393e59c943d6a75a9241140faca326501f792f05

https://foreignpolicy.com/2017/11/28/
the-quantum-gap-with-china/

[79] "Is China the Leader in Quantum Communications?", Inside Science, January 19, 2018

https://www.insidescience.org/news/
china-leader-quantum-communications

[80] "Peace in our Time", Neville Chamberlain, 1938

http://www.digitalhistory.uh.edu/
disp_textbook.cfm?smtID=3&psid=4060

(A reference to British Prime Minister Neville Chamberlain's much lauded efforts to appease Hitler by giving him the Sudetenland. In the end, the appeasement did nothing but convince Hitler that the West was weak and he could easily make war.)

[81] "Clinton Donors Charged in Massive Campaign-Finance Scheme", Yahoo! News, December 4, 2019

https://news.yahoo.com/
clinton-donors-charged-massive-campaign-131442639.html

[82] "Did This Chinese Billionaire Try to Buy Hillary Clinton and Terry McAuliffe?", Daily Beast, May 23, 2016

https://www.thedailybeast.com/
did-this-chinese-billionaire-try-to-buy-hillary-clinton-and-terry-mcauliffe

[83] "Portland mayor stands by decision to allow antifa to block traffic, hassle motorists", The Washington Times, October 14, 2018

https://www.washingtontimes.com/news/2018/oct/14/
ted-wheeler-portland-mayor-stands-decision-allow-a/

[84] "Five of the Best Examples of Left-wing Bias on Wikipedia in 2017", Breitbart, February 1, 2018

https://www.breitbart.com/tech/2018/02/01/
five-of-the-best-examples-of-left-wing-bias-on-wikipedia-in-2017/

[85] "Do You Trust Snopes? You Won't After Reading This.", Food Babe Kitchen,

https://foodbabe.com/
do-you-trust-snopes-you-wont-after-reading-how-they-work-with-monsant

[86] "Hillary Clinton takes her 'deplorables' argument for another spin", The Washington Post, March 3, 2018

https://www.washingtonpost.com/news/the-fix/wp/2018/03/12/
hillary-clinton-takes-her-deplorables-argument-for-another-spin/

[87] "Obama angers midwest voters with guns and religion remark", The Guardian, April 14, 2008

https://www.theguardian.com/world/2008/apr/14/
barackobama.uselections2008

[88] "Bitcoin couple may face death penalty in Thailand over 'seasteading' effort", Fox News, April 18, 2019

https://www.foxnews.com/world/
bitcoin-thailand-seasteading-american-couple-death-threat

[89] "Corruption Perceptions Index", Transparency International

https://www.transparency.org/en/countries/united-states

[90] "Principality of Sealand",

https://sealandgov.org/

# Index